POOR IN SPIRIT

POOR IN SPIRIT

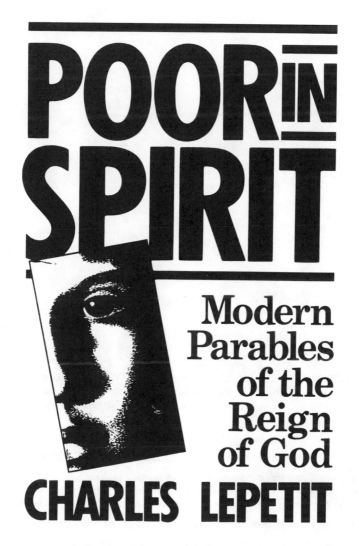

Modern Parables of the Reign of God

CHARLES LEPETIT

AVE MARIA PRESS   Notre Dame, Indiana 46556

Contents

Introduction

After reading my manuscript, the editor said to me, "But your readers won't know who's talking to them. You must introduce yourself."

Of course he was right. I too like to know who is ringing at my door. But... betray my anonymity in the market place? That's not my style.

I am a monk, a member of the Little Brothers of Jesus, a poor disciple of Charles de Foucauld, as I have been nearly all my life. I have lived in slums, I have known hunger, I have been in jail (oh, not for long). I am an invalid. And, I look forward with happiness to meeting the Lord.

And so I am at home with my brothers and sisters the poor. We are of the same cloth, they and I. I had them before my eyes as I was writing every page. They and I speak the same language — the language of facts, the language of simple things of life, the language of the heart.

My sisters and brothers, the poor, would never have thought of writing a book. Nor would I. I was asked to. For over a year I refused. God knows how much I would rather stay the little person that I am in my own little corner of the world. But they insisted. They talked of service. And I capitulated.

This book consists of a series of true stories. Each of them has been confided to me, for you, by someone poor. I have demanded no other "I.D." of my heroes. They are hungry, they are marginalized, they are handicapped. They make a living by working too hard.

But they all have one poverty in common: that of the heart. They do not know the treasure they bear.

How did I set about it?

I had neither the money nor the time nor the health to go scampering about the globe. So I wrote letters to some poor friends.

The majority of these friends are members of religious orders, disciples of Charles de Foucauld, even as I. They belong to different branches of his spiritual family, but have all made certain choices in their hearts about how they approach human beings and God. You will soon realize what I mean.

Some of my correspondents have opened their own hearts to me. Others have led me to the heart of someone close to them.

Some sent me a manuscript practically ready for publication. Others replied, "Ask me questions, anything you want. I'll answer. But do the writing yourself!"

And so, thanks to this exchange of letters, I have managed to focus the camera of my heart more and more precisely on this woman and that man, on their trailer, their shack, their bus. I wanted to make you see them as if they were right in front of you.

The style of the stories that I have had to compose myself is unpretentious. I have made no attempt to create literature out of someone else's poverty. I have sought only two things: simplicity and scrupulous accuracy in every detail.

Each story is independent of the others. They are presented to you in quite an arbitrary order.

None will deal primarily with the organized struggle of the poor. The domain is too vast, and others have told you about it already.

The forename after each story will indicate only whether the writer is a man or woman. Nothing more.

The stories are a kind of parable. Like those of Jesus, they evoke in one way or another the Kingdom of God hidden among us.

They are meditations. They are worth stopping and thinking about.

Take my word for it! It has taken me quite a while to come to see Mary, Martin, Margaret, Harry and all the others take shape before my eyes. From one detail to the next, they have become altogether real and familiar to me, along with all the other characters in their stories. I carried them about with me, living in their shadow. We have become friends.

Without my being aware of it at the time, something has passed from them to me. Each of them has bequeathed me, discretely, a pearl of the Kingdom. Since then I have not been quite the same fellow.

How could I not wish you to have the same adventure as I?

Will you live for a while with Mary, Martin, Margaret, Harry and the others? Might they become friends of us both?

One more thing. Do not forget to extend your hands.

Put out your hands? Yes. Empty hands. A beggar's hands. Forgetting everything you think you know or own.

Could our friends put a pearl in a hand filled to overflowing?

1
Morning Psalm
Black Africa

The loudspeaker exploded with a roar into my bedroom. I awoke with a start. I didn't have to look at my watch to know it was 4:30 a.m. It was the hour of the first call to prayer at the mosque.

They were crazy to wake us up at that hour. It had been so hot that night that I had not got to sleep before 1:30 a.m. What a way to treat a person!

I must have dropped off for I have another start: that loudspeaker again! 4:45. Fine! Still not for me. The mosquitoes danced around the mosquito net. I hadn't the strength to open my eyes. I dropped off again.

Punctually the shrill voice wrenched me once more from my rest. I still needed at least another good hour's sleep, but it was no use. I stayed awake.

Everything was still.

A moment of silence is rare in our neighborhood. I savored it.

I thought of Grandfather next door. He would be unfolding his old body and getting up to go to mosque.

And my young neighbor, as tired as I. I had said to her: "It's hard to get up when one hasn't slept enough." She had replied: "The first prayer of the day is the only one I can make. During the day I don't have time anymore. Anyhow, you have to start the day somehow. So why not begin it with God? That gives you the strength for the rest of the day."

The loudspeaker interrupted this moment of silence. It coughed, it spat. Somebody was fiddling with a cassette.

This time I felt happy.

I waited for that voice I love at dawn.

There it was, marvelous. No words to describe it.

God is great.

There is no God but God.

He is the Merciful One.

Come and pray!

The chant went right through me. It became a prayer in me.

The voice fell silent, plunging the still young day into peace.

I noticed the first signs of awakening life: the crackling of a wood fire, a pail being pulled from the well, the rhythmic blow of the pestles pounding millet in the mortars, the scuffling of a little branch broom.

It matters little whether I'm awake or asleep, cheerful or downcast, I love this hour of hope each morning. It's like a psalm springing from life's familiar sounds. It opens to me a day, given by God.

I got up. I still had an hour before going to Mass. I prolonged this morning psalm in prayer.

The day dawned. I left for the church, ten minutes away, along the wide, red-clay street which was deserted at that hour. Instinctively I followed the winding path which made its way between mounds and hollows.

Every day at exactly the same spots I pass men coming back from the mosque. Most are old. Their walk and a little breeze in their long, full clothes give them a majestic air.

We come up to each other and exchange greetings:
"May God receive your prayer!"
"May your day pass in peace!"
"May God come to your help!"

This morning ritual is more than a habit. It has become a necessity. It prolongs their prayer at the mosque, and leads into my Eucharist.

The psalm goes on...

Catherine

2

The Cassette

North America

Pablo half-turned and nodded toward the window. From the fourth floor I looked down onto the street with him.

Some young junkies were tripping. They were leaning against the walls and doors of the houses. Some of them would stagger, fall and then get up again, shakily. Across the street, on the first steps of the stone staircase of the house, some men who were still young were dozing. Once in a while they would take out a bottle for a swig.

Pablo turned to me and said, in jerky English, "For kids... the city... no good."

I had just asked him when his family would be coming to join him. They were still in Latin America. Now I knew why. He preferred to stay here alone rather than expose his children to what we had just seen.

In fact, I did not know him yet. We both worked in a school. His job was maintenance, looking after the heating system and such. I was the "cleaning lady."

It had started with a "Hi" and a "How's it goin'?" Later we saw each other twice a week at the pupils' Mass. During the prayer of intercession Pablo would raise his arms to heaven. Eyes wide open, he would pray aloud, in Spanish, for his family, the people of this country, the other immigrants, and everyone who had helped him find a job.

He attracted and intrigued me. Why not have him over, I thought.

So one day I stopped him in the corridor. "You like going to Mass, Pablo. Why don't you come with me after work one of these days to a church where they have Mass in Spanish. It's right on the corner."

I could see he was embarrassed and hesitant.

So I added, "Perhaps you don't have time." I knew he also worked for a few hours in the evening as watchman in front of a shop. That was not the problem though, he indicated. I was puzzled.

Finally he told me, "Impossible to come. Have to pray. With family."

Pray with his family? I was getting more and more confused. Why couldn't we pray for his family together, at Mass?

He could see I didn't understand. With his serious and slightly sad air, but decisively, he motioned to me to follow him. We made our way along a series of corridors to a door, which he opened. We were in a room where the school dumped everything needed for maintenance, for making recordings, etc.

He led me over to a tape recorder. He gazed at it delightedly, almost with tenderness, and plugged it in. Then he took a cassette out of his left pocket and inserted it delicately into the machine, as if it was the most precious thing in all the world. He pushed the play button.

The room filled with the voices of a woman and several children. They were reciting the Our Father, in Spanish. Relaxed, Pablo listened attentively.

To my surprise the voices fell silent after "on earth as it is in heaven." I looked at Pablo. "Give us this day our daily bread," he said, in Spanish, and finished the prayer. Although he alone replied, he was doing so as a head of family with the tone of one accustomed to leading the prayer. It was like hearing him pray in his own home.

The voices resumed. This time it was the Hail Mary. They stopped in the middle and Pablo finished it.

I was very moved. Now I understood why Pablo couldn't go to Mass with me. His family was waiting for him.

I would have liked to join in the prayer, but my Spanish wasn't good enough. Spontaneity carried the day, though, and I found myself praying with Pablo anyway, in my own language, guided by the alternate rhythm of those far-away prayers and silences.

So, the Communion of Saints uses a tape recorder...

Pablo stopped the machine, and gently removed the cassette.

Then, with a look of pride, he told me, "Every night... the Rosary... my family and I."

We said goodbye.

I went back to my laundry, my mind still far away in Latin America.

Two minutes later I could hear Pablo noisily dragging some big garbage cans out onto the pavement.

Nancy

3

A Perfectly Normal Thing to Do

North Africa

She was a tiny little thing, in her long, brightly, colored cloth, the kind they wear in the countryside. Two expressive eyes sparkled in her wrinkled face. Toil and hunger had aged her before her time.

Her name was Mabruka, "the blessed one."

Slung over her back were two or three large pieces of different colored material serving as sacks. All one had to do was tie the four corners of each piece of material together and slip the knot over one's forehead. That distributed the weight evenly between one's back and head. It was thus that in the past she had carried five gallon drums of water, held by a rope pressed to her forehead.

At day break, each morning, she would come down the mountain to the town with a whole group of women — a walk of about four miles. At the public spring, she had first to fight her way through the arguing crowd, for everyone wanted to be first. Then, bent double under the weight of her filled drum, she would move with a heavy step through the crowded streets to serve her women customers. In those days they did not come out of their houses.

She would knock on a door. A child would open it a crack and then go and tell mother, who would call either, "Tell her to come in!" or, "Not today!"

By noon, Mabruka would have finished her rounds. She and her companions would climb back up the mountainside, with a bit of food bought with the few coins they had earned.

Today everything was different. Now there were water mains, with pipes right into the houses. One after another the springs had been closed. The water-bearers had lost their usefulness.

But Mabruka had three mouths to feed, three little girls she had taken in.

So now she went out begging, every morning, or almost. Above all on Fridays, when prayer and almsgiving are especially recommended in Islam.

She passed through our neighborhood. Everyone was poor there. The men gave a few coins as they left the mosque. The women generally gave something in kind, a bit of couscous, a few pieces of fruit, but mostly, stale bread.

Bread is considered a gift of God here. It commands respect.

Mabruka sold her pounds of hard bread to sheep or chicken farmers. How in the world could she feed her girls with the pittance she earned in that way?

Mabruka had always been frugal. In the part of the country she came from, children learned to go hungry from their earliest years. All their lives they would have only what was strictly necessary, which they would have to share with any passing guest.

Today was Friday. Mabruka stopped at our door and knocked. It was practically a tradition.

I opened the door, and I noticed behind her a young woman whom I did not know, and whom I would never see again. She was begging from door to door, with a large sack on her back. She had seen Mabruka knocking on our door and had stopped.

Mabruka began by blessing me. She knew a whole gamut of blessings by heart.

Generally it was my younger sister who opened the door, but today she was sick and I told Mabruka about it. Instantly she prayed, "God grant her healing and the forgiveness of her sins."

The young unknown beggar had heard all of this, and I noticed her rummaging in her sack. She had just been given two beautiful scarlet pomegranates.

Smiling, without a word, she handed them to me.

Both women left immediately without waiting for anything.

Carol

4

God within One's Reach

Latin America

The priest and I climbed the mountain. Above us bare and timeworn peaks stretched across a gray sky. Everything was soaking wet. One last escarpment, and a vast landscape of mountains and valleys lay before us. Every last bit of arable land was under cultivation. Here and there we could see tiny houses with their thatched roofs, seemingly deserted. Nor was anyone to be seen along the paths furrowing the slopes. The stillness was complete.

From a great distance the priest waved his hat vigorously as a sign of greeting. No response. Yet he had sent word that he was coming.

A little boy in a red poncho had come halfway up the slope to meet us. But he said not a word. The priest asked him to whistle — the kind of whistle you do with your fingers in your mouth — to announce our arrival. He refused, again without a word.

Were they going to accept us up here?

After all, we had come from the village at the foot of the mountain, where the church and cemetery were. The village belongs to the whites — the settlers, the thieves and the priest. The Amerindian is stranger there, scarcely a human being.

There is a bridge at the edge of the village where mestizo traders wait for the Amerindians, to snatch their onions, corn, potatoes, woven ponchos, anything that can be carried down the mountain to be sold in the village. With the few coins they receive in exchange, all they can do is get drunk in the bars. In order to forget.

In the village, Amerindians let themselves be fleeced and insulted.

But up on the mountain, they are King. Here is their fortune, here their fortress. And woe betide the intruder!

Were they going to accept us up there?

We came to a little terrace covered with grass. At one end was a dilapidated chapel. Four walls of dried mud brick, a tile roof and, in the wall facing us, a niche which had once contained a bell.

The clouds swept by at ground level and the damp enveloped us.

A little shepherd boy came up with his sheep. Then a man, and, soon after, another. Each carried a hoe over his shoulder. A moment later, a group of five men emerged from a path, their hair plastered down on their foreheads with sweat. They had been moving through the mountain since five o'clock that morning, spreading the word of our arrival. Yes, they assured us, the others were on their way. This was the first time they would have seen a priest up here. And he wasn't asking to be paid.

Yes, they were going to accept us up here.

Sure enough, wisps of color began appearing down the paths. The little yard in front of the chapel would soon be full of men and women, sixty of them. It looked an artist's palette. Bright blue trousers and red ponchos on the men, and black or navy-blue skirts on the women, with great purple shawls fastened across the chest. But mud, everywhere.

Children, sheep, and dogs edged into the group. There was even a little black pig among our number.

At one p.m. everybody entered the chapel.

What poverty! Two tiny square windows and the brown walls and floor bathed us in a mysterious half-light. The pungent smell of cow and sheep made do for incense.

We spread out a poncho over a sort of stretcher that must have been used to bear Mary in procession on feast days. This would be the altar. Everyone pressed around it. A single candle lit up the nearest faces from below, accentuating their rough features. The chalice and hosts to be blessed were brought up.

The priest began to speak, taking a passage from the Lord's prayer as his text. The words touched his hearers' hearts, and a spark was lit. A dialogue began.

God seemed to lose his "foreign" face and become someone well known in their mountains.

The priest began the Eucharistic prayer. He spoke the words of blessing, and prepared the people to receive communion.

Communion? Down in the village, Amerindians never go to communion, except for First Communion and for their own weddings, and even then only because they have to.

So the priest explained that Jesus was not here for the just, but for sinners.

That was when it happened. It was totally unexpected, and totally spontaneous.

All of a sudden there was a rush.

First for the hosts.

The glow of the candle intensified the gleam in these hungry eyes, greedy for the sinners' bread. Fearlessly, all helped themselves.

The hosts were not enough, so they descended on the chalice. It wasn't designed for the kind of gulps they were taking and I can still hear the priest saying, "Easy, easy!"

The noise of a tightly packed little throng...

Everything was topsy-turvy in this chapel of the Andes. God was suddenly Amerindian, in a church as poor as the thatched huts of the people. He had put himself within their reach!

Everyone recognized Him.

Frances

5

"What about Sahin, the Turkish lathe-worker?"

Northern Europe

Was it coming off or not? My safety helmet, I mean... I was suspended head downward, twenty feet up.

My lower half was stretched out over the platform of the mobile crane. The only way I kept my balance was by wedging my left foot against a bar of the guard-well.

I pushed the handle of my grease pump with my right hand. But as the gasket was worn, I had to press it with my left hand in order to insert the grease into the wheels of the crane. I needed both my hands at the same time. Not bad acrobatics.

Down below was the usual din. We had to bellow to be understood, just from the noise of the machines. But worst of all were the "bangs," regular and deafening. The sparkling yellow ingots, just out of the furnace launched themselves against the draw-plates. The shock was terrible. Then the next draw-plate, a little smaller, and another "bang"!

Moving from plate to plate, the blinding metal was transformed into wire four one-hundredths of an inch thick, for reinforced concrete. It cried out, creaked and writhed. And right below me it hissed like a snake as they sprinkled water to cool it.

I pulled back from my precarious position in mid-air to stretch full length on the platform for a few minutes. The rim of my hard hat kept my nose out of an inch-deep layer of filings. My overalls would have such a coating of grease and filings after two hours on the job that they could have stood up by themselves.

Stunned with fatigue and noise, I still had a whole day of grease-pumping in front of me.

It was at times like these that I asked myself: "What the hell am I doing in this pile of crap?"

I pulled myself up, backed down the ladder, and headed for the machine shop to refill my pump again.

I found Pauli there, working his lathe.

We were both on the Workers' Council. I was still a "new-boy." I didn't find it easy to feel at home among my mates on the Council, or to get used to the regulations and tricks of the trade. Apart from us, the Council members took a pretty casual attitude.

And this atmosphere was getting me down. There were going to be forty lay-offs, mostly Turks. Our country had enjoyed a period of economic growth, and legal aliens had come in to do the hard or dangerous jobs. What should we do to prevent these mates of ours from being sent back to their country against their will? Nobody on the Workers' Council spoke Turkish, hence my concern about the future Council elections.

"Seen the goodbye list for Friday?" I asked Pauli. I showed him the sheet with all the Turkish names.

He reacted in his usual impulsive fashion. He shouts a lot, even for a joke, but he's straight. "I couldn't care less, as long as they're Turks."

"Come on, they're our mates. Out of the hundred and eighty workers here, a hundred are foreigners. They should have a representative, don't you think? What would you think of Sahin, the Turkish lathe-worker?"

"No way," Pauli replied, decidedly but without animosity. "Besides I'd be astonished if the union would agree to it."

I didn't answer. Feeling very sad, I climbed back onto my crane with a full grease pump.

I remembered some graffiti in the factory yard: "Hang the foreigners!"

No kidding, what was I doing in this pile of crap?

The forty lay-offs took place.

Nine months passed. I felt more at home on the Workers' Council now. I did what I could to defend the interests of my mates, fellow citizens or foreigners. Not that it was a simple matter. They were all afraid for their jobs. And the Turks "are stealing our jobs!"

I was with Pauli again in the workshop. We were talking once more about the upcoming elections.

"What about Sahin, the Turkish lathe-worker?" he said. "He'd be good, don't you think?"

I looked at him astonished, full of joy. I was speechless.

Back onto the crane.

What was I doing in this pile of crap? I had just received a smidgeon of an answer. Just a spark, that was all. But it did me good.

Martin

6

The Cry

North America

I was nearly twenty.

That Sunday evening, for the first time in my life, I had refused to accompany my mother to Mass. Something had just snapped between us.

I went up to my room, feeling desperately sad. My parents' suffering crucified me, for I loved them more than anything in the world. Everything beautiful that I had discovered in life I had found in my family. It was thanks to them also that I had been able to go to secondary school. My father was a miner.

Secondary school was where my life had fallen to pieces, when I was about fifteen. The values of the consumer society were supreme there. Hardly anyone in school cared about God. Everything that I thought beautiful and that I accepted without questioning was turned upside down.

All at once church ceased to mean anything for me. The services seemed cut off from life. I found Christians leading comfortable lives, remote from real problems.

I really wouldn't wish the anguish of my searchings on anyone.

Not believing in God anymore.

Not knowing why I was alive.

Living for myself alone, walled up in myself.

Condemned to grope in the dark.

For years!

The only thing that still impressed me was the example of certain committed workers. At least they were still on fire for their fellow workers.

And one little sentence from a priest. I had said to him, "The Gospel's very beautiful, even if it's just a fairy tale." That had hurt him. And he had written to me: "Jesus has seized hold of me."

I had to find a way out of this and make a choice.

I would find out whether the Gospel was true or not on judgment day. If Jesus existed — a nostalgic notion as far as I was concerned that could only be a pleasant surprise. Meanwhile, I couldn't live on illusions.

Because it was a question of how I was to live, I would follow the example of those committed to the service of others.

But that would not be within the Church anymore.

If I left it, it would be in order to be true to myself.

And so, that Sunday evening my poor mother set out for church alone. Broken by this separation, I said a sort of prayer by the edge of my bed before stretching out.

Suddenly, a cry erupted in the depths of me.

It was so loud I thought it must have been heard throughout the room. But — I cannot say how — I sensed that the cry had been only inside of me.

It was a cry of suffering, anguish and agony.

The cry of someone who loved me to the point of madness, and who was appealing to my tenderness.

At the heart of the cry, I heard my name, pronounced with extraordinary precision.

I recognized straight away the voice of the One I had been looking at from afar without recognizing Him.

My first reflex was a woman's. I opened my arms as if to embrace someone I loved who was weeping.

He who I thought had disappeared rushed into them like a beggar. He let himself be consoled by me, who was so poor in love, so lost in the face of suffering.

I was convinced of the *presence* of *somebody* at the deepest point in myself. I have no words to express it.

That cry of Jesus could have killed me.

Truth is like a flash of lightning.

But Jesus is the gentlest, most human being I have ever met. He is the humblest, and the poorest.

I shall never forget the tenderness of that cry. Everything could crumble around me (and how many failures have I tasted over the past eighteen years) and that cry would still resound, just as it had done that evening.

It was all over in a fraction of a second.

I lay awake the rest of the night.

Several years later, I left for a Third World country. I wanted to proclaim to the poor that Jesus was alive.

And the poor found their way into the depths of my heart, one by one, each in their own unique way.

Then I heard that same cry again, coming this time from all the poor.

Through the face of each one of them, Jesus was begging for my tenderness again. "You did it to me " (Matt 25:40).

I had come to understand that He was "in agony till the end of time."

Lucy

7

Has God an Address?

Southeast Asia

I recently paid a visit to the overcrowded neighborhood where Weï Ling lives. It's a collection of gigantic blocks, all painted in mournful, washed-out colors. Some five thousand people in each block!

I began by lining up at the elevator and finished by stepping out on the 18th floor into an endless corridor.

Immediately my ears were assaulted by a diabolical racket: radios turned up full blast, children crying, adults arguing, and mah-jong tiles (Chinese dominoes) clicking.

The only note of sweetness in the air was a soft, perfumed smoke rising from incense sticks burning near the doorways. This popular practice is to call down the protection of the gods and ward off evil spirits.

What a corridor! A real prison corridor, dark, in bare concrete, lined with heavy sliding iron grilles to guard against theft and violence.

Behind each grille was a wooden door, generally left open because of the sultry heat and stuffiness. Each led into a single room, twelve or so feet square, with a whole family living in it, sometimes as many as eight or ten people.

Down the corridor I went from grille to grille, looking for Weï Ling.

Finally there she was, a short little woman, a bit on the heavy side, with close-cropped black hair. Peace, simplicity, joy, and honesty were things I noticed straightaway in her look. She was dressed simply in a blue cotton jacket, trousers of matte material and a pair of plastic slippers.

She had just returned from her day of charring — the family's only source of income — and was making supper in the tiny kitchen that had been set up in a corner on the left side of the narrow balcony. Her elder daughter, aged 14, had done the shopping. The two boys were still out, and the husband would be loitering somewhere. He didn't work, he gambled, and of course lost.

Everything was clean and neat. Two metal bunk beds stood in each corner of the room on the left. In the far right corner was the parents' bed. There was a table and a wooden trunk, with suitcases and boxes under the beds, since there was no built-in cupboard or wardrobe. On the balcony were a few green plants, and laundry drying on bamboo sticks.

Weï Ling cooked for eight mouths, morning and evening. There was the father, two daughters, two sons, herself. Eight persons? There were still two unaccounted for.

In fact, Weï Ling had taken in a cousin of twenty-eight, a mentally handicapped woman whose own family was no longer willing to care for her. At night she slept on a thin mattress that had been rolled out over the concrete floor.

On the floor? Was there not room for a bed in the corner to the right of the door? In fact, there was one there. Weï Ling had learned that a young polio victim in the neighborhood, aged 22, had been shown the door by his parents because his illness caused them to "lose face." He had spunk though, and earned his own living.

Weï Ling had gone to see him and had offered him a place in her room. To her, it went without saying. "I couldn't leave that boy on the pavement, could I?"

And so, in the corner on the right, alongside the bed where the cousin used to sleep, they had put a sort of laminated screen so that the young polio victim would feel at home. As for the cousin, she slept on the floor.

A few days before my visit, Weï Ling, who practiced no formal religion, confided to a woman friend of mine a great anxiety of hers concerning one of her daughters. And she added: "Pray for us. I cannot read or write. I am useless, good for nothing. But you are a Christian. You know how to speak to God."

Weï Ling thinks she cannot reach God. And yet it is she who has shown me where God lives, and how to find Him.

She has shared a secret with me. It is a secret she lives on without knowing it.

It is a secret that God has patiently been striving to make me understand.

A secret which is contained in a single word: "Love!"

"Really love *that* boy, *that* girl, whom I set in your path *today,* at *that* exact spot. You will find me there also: that's my address."

Jim

8
A Can of Milk and Some Dates

Sahara

Everywhere the nomads had been devastated by a pitiless drought. Camels, donkeys and goats dried up in their tracks.

The nomads got to a city any way they could, hoping for help. Those who were too old or too young died by scores along the way. Places where hardly anyone ever came before now saw little groups gathering, by family, around a few wells.

The fifty tents that had been provided by the government had not been enough, so up sprang teetering little shelters, as protection against the wind, sun, and cold. Everything was used — old sticks, cardboard, boxes, brushwood. The shelters might sometimes measure no more than six feet square. Actually this was big enough to fit a family, because no useless baggage was brought along.

These were nomads, and nomads don't like being on top of each other, so the camp was very spread out. It was motley, totally lacking in organization, but clean. Here and there a goat, which had survived the drought — or was a gift from villagers — nosed among the refuse.

29

Relief efforts were inadequate at first, and there was no wood for cooking. Everyone went hungry.

I remember one evening in a tent. There were four children, ranging in age from perhaps six or seven to twelve. They were weeping with hunger, and begging, "Papa! give me something to eat!"

I can still see the father, his handsome face a bit weary, but peaceful. He spoke to them. "Ah, my children, do not weep! Did not God send us a bit of bread this morning? Let us thank him. Tomorrow, as soon as the shops are open, I shall go begging for you. I'll bring you a can of milk and some dates."

And he went on and on, telling the children of better days to come, until they calmed down and fell asleep.

The mother prayed, "Lord, have mercy on us. Thou knowest everything. Thou canst do everything. Fill our needs. Praise be to Thee!"

Often these nomads slept on empty stomachs. There was not much conversation those evenings. When we took leave of one another, we would say, "Until tomorrow, and let us hope it is a good day!"

Then they would make their Muslim prayers, while I drew apart to pray in my way.

I fell asleep under the stars.

The morning is the moment of grace. The first faint glimmer of new day, and my neighbor awakened me softly: "Get up and make your prayer!"

The nomads were already prostrating themselves toward Mecca at the entrance of their shelters. "In the name of God the Compassionate, the Merciful... Praise be to God, Lord of sky and earth! Thee only we worship, and to Thee do we cry for help. Lead us along the path of those who do good!"

And a little distance away I was invoking the thrice-holy God: "Come, let us adore the Lord. Glory be to the Father, and to the Son, and to the Holy Spirit, as it was in the beginning, is now, and ever shall be, world without end. Amen."

After our prayer, each of us kept silence, even while doing some kind of work.

Moment of contemplation, hour of hope! We were not yet thinking about what awaited us during the day. We were simply thankful for the new morning. And what a beautiful morning it was!

Day broke gradually, tiptoeing through every hue of the rainbow. The sun's rays could be seen from behind the mountain. It broke free and its first warmth was a blessing after the cool of the night.

Immediately the camp sprang to life.

Those who had found, or hoped to find, work for that day left at once, just as they were, without even a drink of tea or a bite to eat.

The four children in the tent would be waiting for their can of milk and the dates.

They were resting in the hands of the Merciful One.

Paul

9

With the Gospel on the Table

Latin America

The whole little *pueblo* was there that evening, in the big room with the low ceiling. The cozy light of the kerosene lamp lit up the whitewashed walls.

The people had squeezed onto benches along the walls. Babies slept on their mothers' backs, while the young children played. Very soon, they, too, would be lost to the world, asleep on little mats with their heads on their mothers' feet. The dogs threaded their way between people's legs before settling near their masters.

On the wooden table in the middle of the room were piled songbooks and copies of the Gospels.

The atmosphere was cheerful and familiar. All were happy to see their *padrecito* again (their name, at once respectful, familiar, and affectionate, for their priest). They would be able to keep him for three days!

The latest news of the place mixed with laughter:

"Señora Elena — you know her well — Don Miguel's wife. She's had a boy. Her fourth. Are you coming to baptize him, padrecito?"

"And Don Simon — remember, the one who never took part in the village projects. Well, he fell ill. His field was full of weeds and his onions were going to rot. So we said, you only fight evil with good, and we all went over to work in his field. Don Simon hasn't missed a project since!"

A child begged for a song. He passed out the books himself, and even found the page. We began to sing.

Then Don Pedrito stood up. He was the coordinator, a family man, and full of life. With the help of a small council he was in charge of the little Christian community, because there was no priest in the vicinity.

One of the children passed out the gospel books.

Don Pedrito reverently took off his black felt hat and placed it on the table. He picked up the book of the gospels and announced that he would read the familiar passage on brotherly love that begins with the eleventh verse of the third chapter of the First Letter of Saint John.

Gradually quiet fell. Don Pedrito started to read slowly.

After reading the verses, he put down the gospel book, sat down, and asked: "What does this reading mean to us?"

He gave the first answer himself. "What struck me was verse thirteen. 'You must not be surprised... when the world hates you.' "

"You know what they're saying behind my back. The authorities and the rich think I get paid for being the community coordinator. 'You must not be surprised,' it says. They don't like what we're doing in these meetings!"

Others chimed in. "We ought to all live like brothers."

"He who doesn't love his brother is dead."

"It's easy to light a candle. What's hard is to dig a road. You can light a candle and then go away and forget about it. But when we build a road, we use it, and we don't forget what we did."

"We kill each other when we don't pay any attention to each other, when we don't stick together."

Some spoke up, and their conviction came through in the way they emphasized their words. Others spoke so softly that they had to be asked to say it again. Sometimes everyone burst out laughing.

It was a kind of meditation out loud. Some just re-read one of the lines from the passage from John, without comment.

The phrases they used seemed so simple. But it was like the tip of an iceberg: a whole lifetime would be hidden in a single word.

At times, we were surprised, at others strengthened in our faith, just because a certain person said this or that, or said nothing at all.

Don Pedrito continued his questioning. "Are there other ways we can kill each other?"

"With our tongue."

"Slandering others."

"We can also kill each other by ambition."

"Someone who has a lot and doesn't help a person in need."

The meditation progressed step by step.

"We were dead before, because we didn't have the light of the gospel. Now the authorities want to start killing us all over again."

"What should we do?" asked Don Pedrito.

"The light of the gospel has helped us see that we can think, speak, overcome our ignorance and claim our rights."

"We got together and started a village hall. Now we should get together and finish it."

Toward midnight we grew weary. We had all put in a full day's work before coming here.

Don Manuel, our host, came in with a bucket of maize beer. He stopped in front of each of us, filled the cup and offered it to those who were thirsty. We joked while waiting our turn.

It was time to close the meeting. We decided to work together in Don Pedro's field next day. We also decided to accompany Don Pablo to get a land title for one of our number.

We ended with a hymn to our Lady of Good Hope. Then we went out into the mist, the mud, and the night.

Madeline

10

A Calendar on the Wall

Europe

I'm twenty-four years old and I am writing this to you from jail. I desperately lacked affection when I was young. The arguments between my parents were sometimes so serious that I took fright and fled the house for a few days. I'd steal food from stores.

This lack of tenderness later led me to take drugs. But I have broken that habit after seven months in jail.

I simply decided to live with this huge need for affection in the depth of my heart and hoped that time would heal it.

I landed a job in a factory. I had some responsibility and I liked it a lot. My boss would tell me I was like a son to him. I trusted him one hundred percent, even though he never paid me what he'd said he would and wouldn't sign a contract. He said he had financial difficulties, and I believed him.

That is, until the day he fired me, without a word of explanation or a cent of back pay. The union couldn't do anything, since I didn't have a written contract. They explained to me that the boss was mentally ill.

A violent hatred for this man drove me to take revenge and to get what I was owed by burgling his house and other places.

For thirty months I stole.

Morally speaking, the first ten months were not difficult. It was like a game. I thought money would be the solution to all problems. I felt as if I were travelling a wide road, lit from behind by a projector. The farther I went the broader and brighter it became.

But during the last twenty months I suffered terribly. I realized the trap I'd fallen into: after all those burglaries there was no way I could stay out of the clutches of the police. Nevertheless, nothing made me stop. A voice inside me kept saying: "Why stop now? They're going to get you sooner or later. Enjoy life while you are still free!"

I started living in constant fear of the police, day and night. I'd jump three feet every time the doorbell rang. Instinctively I'd keep away from any policeman I saw on the street. I couldn't even look other people in the face, so much did I feel that my burglaries were written in big red letters on my forehead. I didn't talk any more and hardly ate. I'd wake up in the middle of the night with nightmares.

The day they arrested me I felt as if a huge weight, which had been growing heavier for twenty months, had been lifted from my shoulders.

And here I was again, surrounded by four walls.

Only then did I begin to realize how much evil I'd done, and how long I'd be in jail. For the first two days I did nothing but cry. I couldn't understand what had happened to me. I wanted to kill myself.

A biblical calendar was hanging on one of the walls of my cell. It said Jesus had come to save the lost (Lk 19:10).

As I had nothing to lose, I knelt down, crying, praying, only out of despair and without faith. I said to God, "If you're living and ready to help those who are lost, as this calendar says, come and show yourself to me."

I can't exactly explain what happened next during this prayer. It was as if an invisible hand grabbed all my suffering and gave me a brand-new heart. I felt a peace that I had never felt before. I couldn't understand this sudden change.

From that moment on, I couldn't deny the existence of God. Immediately I asked the warden for a Bible, in order to learn how to get to know God.

More and more I was sure of one thing: I was going to have to confess all my offenses. And not just the ones for which they had evidence to squeeze a confession from me. This is what I did, and it hurt a lot. But afterwards I jumped for joy in my cell.

I felt great remorse when I thought of all the people I'd burgled. God made it quite clear to me that, in order to be forgiven, I had to write a letter of apology to each one.

So far I've had over thirty replies and everyone has been extremely nice.

"We don't hold it against you, although the blow made us lose a few nights' sleep." "I have withdrawn the complaint I had filed with the police." "Come and see us when you get out. There's always a place for you at our table."

At Christmas I got about ten parcels from the injured parties.

Today I no longer regret the trial of being in prison. It's no longer a trial, for it is where God has given me a chance to feed on His word.

I've been in "preventive detention" for ten months now, and it's been the happiest time of my life.

It hurts less to have your body than your consciousness in prison.

My aim now is to bring this discovery to others who haven't yet made it.

Kevin

11

Port of Hope

Latin America

We had weighed anchor, and the tramper was steaming at fifteen knots, under a glowering tropical sky.

"Hey, I want to ask you a question." It was Johnny, one of the ship's engineers, who accosted me on the aft deck. Johnny was half English and half Malaysian, with a very dark complexion. A little shy, even self-effacing, he had something dignified and serious about him.

"Can one marry a prostitute?"

"Are you serious? Or is it just a passing fancy?"

"It's serious. I've been to see her the last two times we put in."

"A prostitute's a person," I said. "If you love her, why not?"

"I'm not sure. You ought to see her."

"Okay. Next time we put in."

In those days we were shuttling between Argentina and Alaska, and every couple of months or so we would put in at this little port, the poorest in the world. Except for dock work, the only way to make a living was prostitution.

So two months later we were back. Johnny and I took a taxi one night to Melba's house. On foot you ran the risk of being set upon. Out in the street there was nothing but mud and night. You could hardly see the shacks. Here and there a colored light would indicate a sailor's dive.

Johnny opened the door without knocking. A bare bulb lit the room. There was a table, a couple of chairs. Some kitchen utensils. That was it. On either side of the room was a bedroom; two other prostitutes shared the same house.

Johnny was forty, Melba nearly twenty-eight. She had black hair, a sunburned complexion, and a lively look on a thin face with a slender nose. There was something refined about her. She had four children (all of them fair, by four different sailors, Johnny had told me), whom she had entrusted to a family to look after.

We had a beer and, not knowing quite what to say, we talked ships.

But Johnny was eager for me to talk to Melba. "This one here is a friend of mine. I want you two to talk. You can trust him. He'll explain everything to you." Johnny knew no Spanish, the language of his beloved.

The other two prostitutes didn't budge, so Melba and I went into the next room. As best I could I transmitted Johnny's declaration of love. Melba avowed the same sentiments, and not just because Johnny was already giving her half his income for the kids.

We decided more time was needed. And we sailed away.

"You know," Johnny said to me with his usual calm, "If we marry, I'm determined that she should stop being a prostitute. But when I'm away, do you think she'll be able to hold out? Tell me straight if I should marry her or not!"

We put into port again and I saw Melba again. Here, I felt, was a woman who had been hurt. She'd already had so many promises from sailors! Was this just another affair? And yet she loved him.

On both sides, then, there was genuine love. But it was a love tinged with fear. Was it possible to be faithful with two such professions?

A sudden inspiration told me I had to trust Johnny and Melba.

And so, seated there at the table, they both said yes, very simply and without great emotion.

"And now are you going to make your love official, or are you going to live it in secret?" I asked. Then I learned that they were both Christians, and that they wanted to be married in the church. I promised to arrange it.

Two more round trips. The next time we put in, we would have the wedding.

We came back from up north loaded with railroad cars. Evening came. Johnny had left the engine room. I was still on the windlasses, trying to let my cars down without damaging them. It was spectacular. But the only thing I wanted to do was get the heck out of there and catch up with Johnny!

Night fell, and we raced for a neighborhood where the boarded shacks were built on piles. I was supposed to meet the priest there, to talk about the wedding the next day.

A dozen prostitutes, all decked out in their Sunday best, of every imaginable color. They alone struck a joyful note in that gray, muddy, rainy scene. They were Melba's friends. She had told them she was going to be married "as soon as they get here." When I told them the wedding was not to be until the following morning, they left disappointed. They would have to be sleeping then.

Next day, just before nine, Johnny and I were at the church. It was still raining.

Melba wasn't there. Panic! We rushed round to her house in a taxi. Nobody there! Finally she arrived, forty-five minutes late. She had only been... having her hair done!

The Mass was one I'll never forget. Everything about it could have thrown you into despair. The gloomy, sorrowful, mildewy atmosphere of a church worn away by rain, and nobody there but us four, the priest, Melba, Johnny and I.

Here before me, right up at the altar, were two poor
creatures, alone in life. They could scarcely understand each
other's language. Little by little they had grown to trust each
other. Now they were placing their love in the hands of God.

What madness! But so beautiful.

After the ceremony we went for a drink in a nice café with
some of Melba's friends.

Johnny left the ship that day, while I went back on board
alone.

Five years later I put in again. Johnny and Melba had bought
a little farm far away from the port. They had the four kids with
them.

Alan

12

Testament

North Africa

It was dusk. Both of the buses which made up the regular service had stopped. The flooded *wadi* had overflowed the road.

The driver of the first risked the crossing and made it.

So the second driver decided to give it a try. The current was more violent from moment to moment. Three-quarters of the way across, the bus was swept off the road and turned over onto the bed of the *wadi*.

The passengers struggled to escape in the dying light.

All would get out alive but one woman.

She was a foreigner, a Christian nurse who had settled in this Islamic land twenty-two years before.

Three months earlier, she had written a message to some young Christians. Here is how it ended:

> I wanted to tell you,
> you who do not know the world of Islam,
> what strength it gives me

to live in communion
with a nation of believers.
I have the good fortune through my work,
to live with people who are poor and simple
who all have a deep faith in God,
faith a bit routine at times, perhaps,
but how little it takes
for that faith to be rediscovered,
and deepened.

I cannot tell you how much I,
as a Christian,
am thrown back on my deepest calling
by these people who cry God to me
all through the day.
How many good wishes I hear
in the course of a working day!
Greetings which are never the same.
Nor are these wishes for me alone.
They embrace all those who are dear to me,
those who are close to me,
my family.
They are very deep wishes.
And in my heart, sometimes right out loud moreover,
I answer,
Let it be so! Amen!

Susie

13

Antelope with Mashed Banana

Black Africa

I must tell you about our recent trip into the forest with four Pygmy families, twenty or so people in all, including grandparents and babes-in-arms. It was a short day's march from the village.

As soon as we arrived at the camp, the women built the two of us a little hut of leaves, in a row with the six that were there already and that only needed to be straightened up a bit.

Next morning we left with the women to fish in the river. Single file, we plunged into the forest along impossible paths. You had to watch where you stepped, what with all the trunks and roots and battalions of ants. The scenery was always the same — gigantic trees, luxuriant undergrowth, and sometimes bogs you had to march through in mud up to your knees.

Our Pygmy friends didn't miss a thing, not a single animal track, not a bird call indicating where there might be some honey. We picked caterpillars, mushrooms, anything edible and wrapped them in leaves.

When we got to the river the women split into two groups. We went with the four younger ones.

It was the dry season, and the water was low. Using branches and the clay earth, we began to build the main dam, which would stop the current. Then we went downstream, building new, smaller dams every so often in shallow holes. The trick now was to remove the water with big leaves. Then the only thing you had to do was gather up whatever you found, fish, shrimps, crabs or eels.

We were still beginners, but our companions encouraged us. The work is hard sometimes, but you're standing in cool water in the shade of the forest.

Mothers with babies at the breast had entrusted them to young girls, who carried them about on their hips. When they cried, the girls would comfort them by singing. Their songs gave us a little courage too, as we cleaned the fish. And as we cleaned ourselves! You should have seen us!

Now we had put the fish in little baskets, and so, back to the camp! We had difficulty in keeping up, but the women waited for us. We were back before nightfall.

Two pleasant surprises awaited us.

A man had harvested some wild honey. Naturally he shared it. Marvelous! Another had caught an antelope in one of his traps and was carving it up, under the watchful eye of the children. It went without saying that he would give the giblets, tripe, and certain less choice pieces to those who happened to be there.

But don't think the work was all finished! The fish still had to be smoked over a grill of woven branches. So the women went after wood and started the fires while the children fetched water from the spring, the pans on their heads.

Another nice surprise when we entered our hut. The fire was going! It must have been our neighbor Inoli. And she already had enough to do with all her family!

One gift after another came to us. The young girl of our next door neighbors brought us mashed banana and some antelope in a savory sauce. The gift of a meal always means the best pieces, and is attractively served. Our mashed banana was wrapped in a leaf and put on a plate, even though it could have been the only plate the family had.

We hadn't finished the meal when the little boy from the farthest hut came too, with a plate of fish.

Both children left the way they had come, without a word. It was all so natural.

Everything is shared, you see: banana, fish, honey, antelope, fire. For the Pygmies, a good person is "one who shares" and a bad person is "one who refuses." Do you have something and others have seen it? Then you have to share it. Even with the children it's automatic.

In earlier times this sharing was regulated down to the last detail: so much for the family, so much for one's brothers, so much for the in-laws, and so on. Transgressions were punished. For hunters, it was a matter of life and death.

But then along came money. The numbers of hunting guns multiplied. Merchants set themselves up. Rivalries became more acute, along with the appetite for individual gain.

Some time ago, I was talking to our "elder," the one in charge of the four families. I said: "It's not the way it was, is it?"

"People are still the same," he answered. "Even in days gone by there were selfish people who tried to hide their spoil so that they would not have to share it. Others by contrast, gave you more than they had to. It all depends on your heart."

Night fell. It was a pleasant moment. Everyone reclined around their little fires, each with their own family, happily chatting. They would call from hut to hut and go visiting. This was the time for the old stories, too.

Finally conversation died away. Some one or other would ask God for food for the morrow. Singing, a mother rocked her crying baby.

Then human beings fell still. Nothing could be heard but the thousand noises of the intense life of the forest.

Nicola

14
The Olive Tree in the Crevice
Sahara

It is as if the sun and moon rose and set just for me, in this lonely corner of the world.

While the days pass happily here, other people are working themselves to death for a miserable pittance, the unemployed go from door to door looking for work, prisoners are separated from those they love and some are tortured. Many go hungry on a heartless earth, and innocent people are caught in the crossfire.

My withdrawal into this desert would be intolerable if I were not seeking the loveable face of the thrice-holy God.

I do it for those very people who toil and suffer. I do it as their delegate, taking the place before God, who is their salvation and my own.

And so I strive to behave as if there were no one in the world but God and myself. I speak to Him out loud. I sing to him, I abide in His company, day and night, no matter what I am doing.

There are impressive moments of calm, under a generous sun or a star-studded sky. The occasional braying of a distant donkey hardly reaches me.

In the desert nothing is artificial. Everything seems to exist as if God had just placed it there, without human imprint. The desert seems to draw one automatically towards Truth, Beauty, and Goodness.

Rocks millions of years old, though perishable, speak to me of eternity.

Here it is like being driven back on the absolute essentials. All else crumbles and collapses like a house of cards.

If in this silence I do not feel inclined to listen to God, or to have a little chat with Him, or simply to enjoy His company, then I may as well stay in the hustle and jostling of everyday life. After all, I can find Him there just as well, alongside my fellow human beings and in their eventful lives.

Sometimes I walk and walk along the stony plateau. Other than avoiding stones, there is nothing to distract you there.

And then, suddenly, behind a harsh-looking stone, a flower, radiantly fresh, delicate, smiling, sprung somehow from this dryness.

I sit down, put my elbows on my knees and my hands, under my chin, and my heart has a feast.

The sense of being alone with God is not always discernible and soft. Many a time I will turn my head this way and that to see if there is some living being around me. And sometimes I really desire an encounter, be it just with a snake with which I might occupy myself for a moment or two.

I used to smile in catechism classes when I heard about the Hebrews in the desert sighing for the fleshpots of Egypt. Now I have to laugh at myself, when my body craftily induces images of grocery stores or well-stocked refrigerators!

Everyone can find in the desert an image that will help him or her to better grasp, taste and assimilate the things of the Bible. Walking in the mountains on a bend in the path, I came upon a wild olive tree sticking up out of a crevice in the rock. Now, where could that tree possibly find nourishment and moisture? Its knotted, twisted trunk showed that it had not sprouted yesterday. It looked to have been there forever, impassible and happy at the same time.

Since then I have often happened to read verse ten of Psalm 52: "But I am as a green olive tree that thrives in the house of God: I trust in God's unfailing love forever and ever."

Frank

15

"Stay with us tonight!"

Central America

The hot, humid night was falling all about me. The tropical Central American forest rustled with insects. The moon hid its face behind the heavy clouds of the rainy season. There was a fine storm brewing.

I kept my eyes riveted to the slippery path up the mountainside, where I was climbing, tired, toward the edge of the world.

All at once there it was, that tiny clearing where I came every evening. In it a mudhouse with a tiled roof stood in an enclosure, like an island in an ocean of night.

I opened the wooden gate and crossed the enclosure, with dogs at my heels and the grunting of a pig.

Under the lean-to roof which surrounded the house people were settling down for the night. Hammocks hung everywhere. On the ground under the hammocks lay the less fortunate, squeezed together in the little space which was sheltered from the rain. They drove away a pig, frightening a noisy hen as well.

No one spoke a word. I went into the one-room house, also without speaking. The smoke of the wooden fire, the stench of the pigs, and an odor of general misery reigned in the darkness. From the roof, practically everywhere, hung clothes, hammocks, a few blankets, and some maize, drying.

Thirteen people were squeezed into this twelve-by-twenty-foot room. On one of the two beds lay a mother and her four children. On the other, two women. On the hard dirt floor itself, strips of plastic had been spread out, and everybody had stretched out on them. The owners of the house, who were very poor, were lying alongside the refugees.

I made my way hesitantly in the dark. I might step on a child. It was impossible to recognize the faces.

With the night, the agony returned. To eyes that no longer had any daylight to distract them, the horrible sights began tumbling back, sights that would never be forgotten.

The panic when the first shots rang out, as the soldiers and paramilitary reached the edge of the village. Houses on fire. The husband collapsed in a pool of blood. Three little children with their heads cut off. Corpses floating down the river. A pregnant wife disembowelled with a machete, and the foetus flying through the air, being used for target practice. A frantic flight clutching your baby as tightly as ever you could. And blood, everywhere blood.

There was no way out for these tattered remnants of families. If they were to continue their flight, the soldiers' rifles would be on the lookout for them. If they returned to the village, they would find other rifles waiting.

The endless, agonizing night had begun, a night in which mosquitoes and bugs would never let up.

Everyone had heard me come in, and recognized me, but kept still. I felt a kind of welcome of the heart, warmer than any word could have been. They knew that I was aware of the terrible anguish of their night. They could feel that I wanted to be with them.

I would not be staying long. We all wanted but one thing: sleep.

As I did every evening, I invited them to pray.

"For peace," I said. That's asking a miracle.

"For forgiveness." To creatures who had just been deprived of their last glimmer of hope!

I began a decade of the rosary, one Our Father and ten Hail Marys. The answers came slowly, in a low voice. When we came to the third decade, they started dozing off, and I stopped.

Gently I stroked a sleeping child. I lifted my hand in the dark to say goodbye even though I knew no one could see me, and left in silence.

And there I was back on the path, with my torch, heading for the next house, where I would spend the night.

In their exhaustion the refugees had not spoken a single word to me. But their silence had cried out, "Stay with us tonight!"

During the day I spend my time giving medical assistance, and even more time listening to wounded hearts.

In the evening this silence of ours filled with communion revealed to me one aspect of this tragedy which was taking place on the edge of the world. At this very moment, terrorized by the darkness of night, what these refugees were looking for was the heart of a brother.

Roger

16

My Mother's Blessing

Black Africa

My mother had at last been baptized, a few months earlier.

My father was not a Christian but he encouraged his family to become Christians. And so my mother became a catechumen, when she was expecting me, the last of nine children.

Then my father died. And so my mother suddenly had to provide for her three children alone. Four others had died in an epidemic and two were married. No longer any time for the catechumenate.

My mother took up the fishing trade.

I would still be sleeping when she left each morning, about three o'clock, to join the fishermen on the river. I was afraid for her, every time she left. There were so many dangerous animals in the river, and my mother could not swim.

A boatman paddled her in a dug-out canoe. When she met a fisherman, a long palaver ensued over the price of the fish.

Returning to the bank by dawn, my mother would place her little cloth cushion on her head, and the big round pan, filled with fish, on top of that, and walk to market, which was not just around the corner.

Once in the marketplace, she would install herself in front of her slabs of wood. She would first cut the large fishes into pieces, each to be sold separately. The other fish she would sell in small batches. During vacation time I would sell smoked fish by her side. We were happy to be together.

Every day after school I would pass by the market to see her. She would give me some meal and condiments and, for the sauce, some little fish. Then I would head home to prepare the only meal of the day, supper.

I would put my mother's portion aside, and eat the rest, sharing it with my pals, and we would go and play. But I kept an eye out for my mother, and as soon as I saw her I would return home to serve her the meal.

My mother filled me with good food, and I was at least as well dressed as children who still had a father.

What I loved best at home was my mother's singing. Her laments would bring back the memory of forgotten joy, courage in adversity, or the death of my father. Outside mourning ceremonies, this lament is a mark of loneliness.

One day I confided to my mother that I wanted to become a religious. She did not take me seriously, and attempted to dissuade me. But in time she let herself be won over.

However it could not have been easy. She still had four daughters, yes, but to sacrifice her only son, see him leave for far-away lands, not be able to end her days in his house, which would have been the right way!

She never mentioned this concern to me again.

The day arrived when I was to leave home. I had already said farewell to my mother, as to everyone else. Still, I was missing one thing.

My mother and I strolled toward our hut, chatting.

"Come," she said. "Let us make our last offering to God. My strength is failing. Who knows whether we shall meet again here below?"

We went to her bedroom. Now we were face to face.

Her smiling, pensive, soft gaze fell on me.

She suggested we recite together the Apostle's Creed, the Our Father, and ten Hail Marys.

Then her face took on a solemn look. She began talking to God and the Blessed Virgin Mary.

I wanted to assure her by a word that I was praying with her. But her voice, though calm, had taken a dominant tone. And so I simply prayed with her in silence.

Now, I knew, I would receive what was missing: my mother's blessing. And I bowed my head.

"Be still and listen to me."

Slowly she lifted her arms. Then, in a slow, soft, humble, trustful voice, she asked God to bless us:

> "All belongs to God and returns to God.
> Who am I to oppose your calling?
> Go!
> The greatest riches are not on earth.
> And thanks be to God for having chosen you."

We made the sign of the cross.

Mother did not sprinkle me with fresh water, as one does in a traditional blessing. She omitted this because of the water of my baptism.

Andy

17

Hand upon Hand

India

We were soaked in sweat, though we toiled under the great tree, shaded from the sun.

Face to face, the master carpenter and I were working a long plane. He would thrust it and I would help by pulling. For the assistant, the whole secret is to sense the direction in which the carpenter wishes the plane to move. I was still feeling my way.

My instructor was a person of few words. There were no instructions like, "To the right! Easy does it! Give it all you've got!"

I had to absorb the fine points of my trade simply by watching him do it.

The to-and-fro of the plane became still more hesitant. How was I supposed to pull now? My teacher immediately sensed my difficulty.

Without deeming it necessary to utter a word, he extended his right hand and placed it on mine, at the other end of the plane. With my hand in his, I had only to allow myself to be guided.

The to-and-fro became rhythmic again. Something had been handed on from my teacher to me.

He was a simple, good person. When he saw that I was growing too weary, he would tell me to rest. He treated his customers respectfully.

The business was a small one. There were eight of us: the two brothers who owned the shop, two workers who split the wood, two carpenters, and two young apprentices, of whom I was one. We made beds, tables, stools, benches, and so on. Our shop was as big as the shade of the great tree.

The sun was directly overhead. Time for a break. We sat down on the red earth, in the shade of our tree, on the edge of the road to the big city not far away.

Now, who had invented cars and buses? Each time one of them sped by, we would be engulfed in a cloud of dust. But we did have front-row seats to watch the crowd thronging the road.

At that hour of the day, they were mostly vegetable peddlers, hurrying home with their carts in front of them, and singing, as they did every day, the wonderful exploits of gods and goddesses.

Their songs, almost like recitations, died away in the countryside.

This was when my master joiner liked me to question him on a point of religion, or the great legends. He could discourse on them endlessly. I admired his culture, his wisdom, and his understanding of life.

We finished our lunch and returned to work. And the sweat began flowing again.

I can imagine what a modern manager might say about the way we worked under the big tree.

"Unhealthy working conditions, too many men for the job. Get together to buy a machine, and in a few years you'll have recovered your investment."

And I can already hear my master carpenter's polite reply. "Yes, sir, you are right. But you see, I prefer the peace of nature, and the tap-tap-tap of my adze to the racket of machinery. I take pleasure in seeing the work of my hands."

True, the master carpenter was materially poor. He lived in a little hut fifteen-by-twelve, made of bamboo and palm branch, not a great deal of protection from the icy cold winter. He had but a single piece of material for all his clothing, which he laundered whenever he bathed. He wore neither shoes nor sandals. He barely managed to feed his family, and shared the only plate he had with his wife.

But he had made all his tools with his own hands. And without benefit of electricity! Sitting on the ground with a piece of wood wedged between his feet he could make anything you like, almost perfectly. He was a craftsman and he knew it.

That's where his wealth was.

He would hand it on to his son.

Placing his own hand upon his.

Larry

18

Love's Lament

India

The entrance to a Hindu temple on days of pilgrimage is colorful, noisy, gay and bursting with life. The crowd throngs at the foot of the steps which lead to the sanctuary. The heat of the sun weighs on you like lead.

Sitting in a line of beggars was a man with a weary, swollen face, and a large dressing on his right foot. He had leprosy. His stick lay on the ground beside him, and his bowl was ready for pilgrims' alms. That day they were generous.

Once again he thought over his past... of the day when long, long ago joy had forsaken him... twelve years ago.

I grew up like other youngsters, just as naughty and funny as they all are. I could scramble up a tree like a monkey. Sometimes I would steal sugar cane, and scamper off where I could savor the fruit of my petty thieving.

I was thrashed, too. But I deserved it. My father knew that the divine law was made to be respected. And then, too, he was so nervous, so exhausted from his work as the village blacksmith. Shoe the oxen, shape iron hoops to the wagon wheels, straighten the axles on the carts, and many other things.

I worked with my father. I liked working the iron, being master of my tools, the hammer and tongs, the fire on the hissing forge, and the red hot iron. That was the work of my own hands. I was especially adroit at fashioning ox shoes, and giving them the exact shape of the hoof with a tap-tap-tap on one side and a tap-tap-tap on the other.

My father chose the girl I would marry. She lived in a distant village. She was sweet and good. Her name was Lakshmi. We got married.

I remember every detail of the wedding. Every detail! The clay statue of the god in the court. The garlands, the flowers, the streamers.

The priest who officiated was seated cross-legged, grave, reserved, meticulous. He showed us what to do: take the rice in our bound hands as a sign of fertility; hold this branch and this little coin between our fingers to escape the misfortune of poverty.

Everything is there, in my memory...

Everything is there. And especially the gem that I had to hang around Lakshmi's neck, the neck of my true and beautiful bride who was waiting in silence, with her head bowed. The gem which symbolized our union.

Everything is there. First the stay of a few days in her village so that my new parents-in-law could get to know me and spoil me, as they prepared themselves for the loss of their daughter. Then the return to the village of my childhood, this time with Lakshmi following me as my obedient, devoted spouse.

We had a little boy. How lovely he was! He looked just like the two of us. Like a beautiful, ripe red mango in the sun.

And then that day — it was in winter — when I discovered a numb spot on my arm. Leprosy.

My world fell apart that day.

I came to know the anguish of endless days. I lay awake during long, long nights. You wonder whether there is a curse upon you. You recall everything they say: "It's hereditary, a venereal disease, incurable, voracious."

The nails went into the oxen's hooves less surely now. No longer did I sing to the rhythm of my bellows.

My boy always seemed to be running away from me, and sought refuge in his mother's sari.

There were the increasing demands of Lakshmi, who was faced with debts and declining income.

The leprosy gained ground. There was no longer any hiding my hand which was shrivelling up, or the sores that would bleed when I grasped a hammer, or the burns that I would get at the forge because my hand had no feeling any more.

I had to go to hospital, where my sores were cured.

But when I returned home after two weeks... Lakshmi was gone.

I never saw her again.

That was my night of darkness, thick and unimaginable to anyone who has not known love. Endless as a moonless night with clouds racing beneath the poor light of stars.

Lakshmi did not wish to live with a leper. I understood. The very sight of leprosy is so dreadful. And no one knows how it comes. One must take care.

Lakshmi went away, with our little boy. How I long to see her face again. She wanted to be faithful to the fruit of our love.

I abandoned my smithy. I left the village and the district.

I left like a blind man, lost, alone forever. I became a beggar through village and town.

But Lakshmi is still close to my heart, my eyes and my body. She guides me on my way. She's been there since that day, more present than ever. Twelve years already.

How lovely and good she was!

I live because she lives.

The few coins that I pick up at the temple gate will allow me to think more intensely about the one who is still my wife, my beloved.

Surely, one day I shall find her face once more, transfigured by our love.

Duncan

19

Grandmother's Plate

Southern Europe

I hope my letter won't be too confused. I'm exhausted. It's the flat.

We've already been in this tiny flat for two months and the renovations are still not completed. You can imagine what it's like...

Despite the chaos we had our first Mass, quite unexpectedly. We jammed all the tools and materials into one of the two rooms and had our celebration in the other, you know, the alcove, with no door, the one where everything's in view as soon as you come into the flat.

It was just the priest and us at the kitchen table, but the whole block was there in our hearts. Besides, our next door neighbors were present in their own way: everybody hears everything in these concrete barracks.

Upstairs, supper was over and we could hear the mother shifting the table and chairs in order to unroll the mattresses on the floor. Six pairs of kids' feet were going boomity-boom over our ceiling.

71

Then it was Tarzan. He's the rage of the moment: the kids imitate his voice. Our little Arab neighbor is pretty good at it and he cries to us from the landing. Punctuating our reading of Saint Paul, if you can imagine.

And all this against a background of TV, Arab music, and babies crying.

At the prayer of the faithful we remembered our "Arab Grandfather" in a special way. I don't remember whether I've told you about him. The poor man lost his wife a few weeks ago. He lives right next door in the flat of one of his daughters.

He's an impressive-looking man — tall, dignified, not given to talk, a fur cap on his head, and a mournful look.

The first week we were here he came out quite often, just to look at us, without saying much. He wondered who in the world we could be, and how we could manage as single women.

I told you he recently lost his wife. The Arab neighbors and his whole family came to the wake for two, three, or four days. There wasn't room for them all, so we suggested that five young children come to sleep and eat with us. The family brought over a TV so they wouldn't get bored.

As for Grandfather, you'll never guess what he did.

A few days after his wife died, one evening at suppertime, he opened our door. He was carrying a plateful of mutton couscous.

It was "Grandmother's Plate." It's the custom, anyway among Muslims in Algeria and Morocco, to keep preparing a dead person's meal for forty days. It's given to a poor person, or to someone who prays. It's never thrown away.

You can guess how that moved us.

But to get back to our first Mass. I haven't yet got to the most beautiful bit.

Communion time came. The din outside seemed to dissipate in our hearts, to make way for the Host.

The priest held up the Body of Christ and said the words of the rite: "Happy are those who are called to his supper."

Right at the instant the door opened. It was Grandfather, with the daily plate of steaming couscous. He saw all of us from the door, as we prayed in the alcove, around the table. Without a single word, he set the plate down in the kitchen and left.

We received communion.

Then we shared the couscous.

Molly

20

Praying in the Bus

Southern Europe

A few minutes' walk in the icy winter morning and here I am at the bus stop. The regulars are there. If anyone's missing, we ask, "Is she sick?" or, "Think he might have overslept?"

The bus arrives. The streets are still practically empty at this time, and we roll rapidly through the city. There isn't much talk. Some doze, others read the paper. Some of the women are already crocheting.

Often during this first part of the journey, such and such passage of Scripture comes to mind. It's as familiar to me as the words of a friend. I feel a deep need to come back to it. And if I have something to say to God, I like to use bits from the Psalms.

The bus stops in the main square in front of the station. Everybody there is either getting off or getting on, or waiting for a bus or running for one. I'm getting off. I work my way through wave after wave of the crowd. I can't afford to miss the bus for the factory outside the town.

I get in line. Soon it'll be daybreak. The cold grows more biting. It's the rush hour, and my bus must've been held up. In a few minutes the queue is all the way down the pavement.

There it is. It's already full at the beginning of the route. Nevertheless, other passengers get on at every stop. You're jammed together till you can hardly breathe. Despite this, some of the mothers manage to reach down their babies to nurses waiting at different stops, before continuing on to the factories. Men are in the majority, though.

The bus comes alive. Soccer, politics, elections, neighborhood organizations are discussed. Eventually I manage to work out from the conversations who works in which factory.

I love to pray in the crowd. That's where little springs of prayer well up in me most spontaneously. They don't distance me from the crowd. Far from it. Now, if I have something to tell God, it comes from what I see and hear — struggles, solidarity, injustices, suffering, friendship. It's the crowd that points me towards God.

I get off, my back aching from being shaken about on the bumpy road. Here goes, then, nine hours of work, and standing up!

At six p.m. sharp, as soon as the siren goes, I charge for the changing-room. Only four minutes to make the bus! Otherwise, it means waiting between twenty and forty minutes for the next. And the evening wait is worse. Sometimes the bus is so full, it doesn't even stop.

We're jammed together even more tightly than we were in the morning. The journey seems endless. It sometimes takes a whole hour.

The passengers talk about the day just ended, work, problems, troubles with bosses. They try to help each other figure out what the wording in the work contracts means. That's the big thing these days.

Now my prayer is different.

How can you adore the Lord, sing his greatness and marvels, when your body is broken by work and squashed like a sardine? It's easier, of course, when you're admiring a sunset over the ocean...

What does still well up fairly spontaneously is placing myself before God as the "voice of the others."

On the other hand, it's more difficult to read signs of hope for the kingdom of God in the weary faces of the men and women I'm squeezed up against. And what does my own, equally tired, face say to them? As for believing and for hoping that God is near, well, nothing, or almost nothing, in the daily grind makes it look that way. He seems absent. I could say with the psalmist, "Where is your God?"

Often my prayer is just a sigh, a glance at the One who gives me breath, the One I live for.

This prayer is in the same style as my life: rough, obscure, simple.

Here we are back at the main square. I get off to transfer. Another endless line, and another rush.

You're jostled, you're pushed off balance every time the driver hits the brakes in the evening traffic jams. When you're stuck in one, you suffocate. At this time of the day it often strikes me how drawn and harassed people's faces look.

I spend three hours a day in bus queues and buses. I often feel as if I'm wasting my time. I have so many other things to do! I get impatient. And then, very often, I can't pray.

Such a frantic life doesn't help one to live in the present.

For the Lord, only this instant counts, while I'm worried about the next.

The driver hits the brakes. The bus stops. I'm home.

Teresa

21
The Poor Man, the Fire and Life

India

(Light, sun, fire, and the divine kiss are of great importance in the Hindu religion.)

It was two a.m. on a hot pre-monsoon night. A few heaps of straw gleamed in the moonlight. The deep calm of the little village was disturbed only by the last sounds of a distant revel.

Suddenly a woman's voice, from a neighbor's house, pierced the silence. Loudly it intoned the song of sorrow and love for the dead. A chant almost without melody. There would be a short phrase, followed by a deep intake of breath. Then a gasped cry of despair. Then, abruptly, silence.

It was the voice of Gopal's daughter-in-law.

Gopal, the old, old farmer, had just died.

On and on went the lament, followed by that shattering cry. Her hair undone, dressed in rags, as the funeral rite prescribed, her gestures punctuating her rhythmic chant, Gopal's daughter-in-law would strike her breast, then cast herself headlong onto the blanket that lay over the corpse.

Neighbors and relatives looked on, in silence, under the stars.

79

Gopal, the leper, lay on a bed of straw, under the eaves of the hut. A skeleton. Covered with sores. It had to be seen to be believed.

The Gospel tells us about "losing one's life." Do we know what that means?

Gopal learnt its meaning, day after day. He had lost *everything,* everything that we are accustomed to think essential.

His fingers had gone. His feet had grown numb and bruised by his sores. His sense of touch had faded. He could no longer lift one of his legs, and this had given the farmer's gait a jerky, marionette-like motion. The ulcers had reached his eyes.

He had lost his cows and his fields. The work had become too hard for him, and his two children were not yet old enough to work. He had to hire himself out to a wealthy Hindu in the village.

Years passed. He lost the love of his younger son, who fell prey to the allure of city life and never returned.

He lost the love of his elder son, who began to drink and to beat his father, considering him a useless old burden.

His wife... One evening, when Gopal was bringing in the cows, he found her dead in their hut.

Gopal's heart had kept on beating nevertheless, but in time to a tune which was barely audible.

And yet he had still known how to enjoy life. When rain finally came. Or on his rounds of the rice fields, to make sure the water hadn't broken through anywhere. Or at the sight of the first ears of rice forming.

And you should have seen him beam when he carried his grandson on his hip, with his arm around him!

But his joy was always one without hands, without feet, and without eyes.

He showed gentleness even when he went shouting after the landlord's cows to round them up.

When his daughter-in-law brought him his liquid meals, he would take the bowl in his arm-stumps but never say it was not good or not salty enough.

Sometimes he came over to our house and sat on the floor. He begged to be sent to the hospital, so that he would no longer be a burden to his family. He could not see what he still had to lose. His eyes full of tears, he would sit and wait for hours, only to be told once more that he had his place in the village, that he must stay for his grandchildren's sake, and so on. And then off he would go again, his four-year-old grandson leading him by his little hand.

His suffering is indescribable. But it is written indelibly in heaven.

The day before he died, his grandson had jumped for joy, crying, "Don't be afraid, Grandpa! We'll all go to see you on the pyre!" And Gopal had smiled at him.

He died silently in the night.

But only after having found everything that he had lost.

His elder son cared for him lovingly to the end.

His sufferings, accepted with patience, had become as so many divine kisses to him.

His withered limbs would be able to stretch out in repose, as he lay facing his God.

Now he would be able to set out towards the joy promised him, he who had walked along the paths in such torment.

His ulcerated old eyes were going to open again, to look upon the splendor of the divine sun.

The next morning, relatives took over the song of dead from the daughter-in-law. The sound of them beating their breasts reverberated dully. Their hair was undone.

Then Gopal's body was strapped to a wooden litter and transported to the place where he would be cremated, on the edge of the village.

Everyone came. The slow procession moved off, to the sound of drums and the muffled beating of gongs.

The elder son lit the pyre.

Bright flames enveloped the poorest of the poor.

Steve

22

In Hiroshima by Evening

Japan

I had to be in Hiroshima that evening, for a meeting.

But first I had to finish the day in the workshop, where I operated a drilling-machine. I'd usually do eighteen to twenty-five pieces in a batch, then take a cloth and carefully wipe away the filings, then paint the pieces with a spray-gun.

But over the last three days we'd been working on a special series of compressor parts. Each piece had to be painted immediately after drilling. The boss had personally fitted a little vacuum cleaner onto my drill so I wouldn't have to wipe each piece. And everything had worked fine.

Today it was back to my old batches of normal parts. But, why not use the vacuum cleaner? It would save time. All I'd have to do would be to adapt it to the size of the new series of castings.

No sooner said than done! I gave the wrench one last turn on the nut that held the vacuum cleaner in the right position.

Damn! It didn't work. The hose was too short.

I was starting to get nervous. I could feel the foreman's eyes boring holes in my back. He was obviously swapping opinions with his two benchmates back there a few steps behind me. The noise of my drill isolated me from my fellow workers. There couldn't be any conversation, and I found it difficult to get on with one of the trio.

I walked past them in order to look for an extension hose at the end of the workshop. I caught little snatches of their conversation. "Crazy idea!" "It will only delay everyone's work."

Ought I to have asked them for their advice? It seemed obvious to me that if it worked it would speed things up. And it would mean the end of steel dust getting up your nose.

I walked back past the three pals. They were still watching me and talking, but this time I didn't catch anything. It was too noisy.

I fiddled with my extension hose. I was getting rather nervous. There! That was it. That would work. It had to work. Then they'd just have to shut up.

My hands shook a little as I fixed the bit in the chuck. Those eyes fixed on me...

I set to work. Scre-e-e-ech, and the bit cut into the casting. The little cloud of filings swooshed up the mouth of the vacuum cleaner. It worked!

My first piece was finished. I grabbed the next.

Was it because I was nervous? I had the feeling the others still disapproved of what I was doing.

I had a little trouble centering the second piece. My heart beat faster.

Should I readjust the hoses which were getting in my way? Okay, but make it quick, because there was no slowing down that row of castings. It was getting longer by the minute.

They were still watching me.

I turned my drill back on. Things were starting to go better. One, two, three machined pieces were lined up, waiting to be painted.

My morale was getting higher. And yet I began to feel very sad.

My eighteen pieces were finished. I took them over to the paint bench, grabbed the spray gun, planted myself in front of the pieces, and pulled the trigger.

Over the hissing gun and the humming ventilator I could hear some noise over by my drill, just behind me.

This was no time to look around. I had to pay attention and paint my pieces in rhythmic sweeps so that the paint would go on as smoothly as possible.

I reached the end of the row. A last look over the eighteen shiny new pieces.

At last I could turn around... and I saw red.

There at my drill was the foreman's back. Scattered on the floor were a wrench, the mouth of the vacuum, the hose and the sleeves to join the hoses. The pieces the foreman had just drilled at my bench were covered with metal dust.

I felt as if I were going to explode.

I had to be in Hiroshima that evening.

My God! Would I also be carrying my own bomb?

Lord, have mercy!

I made a dash for the can to keep myself from blowing up. My fists were shaking.

Jim

23

Barefoot Prophet

Latin America

It was the annual patronal feast in a village on the frontier and the bishop was on his way there to celebrate Mass. The journey was not without risk, however, and he would sometimes have preferred to make it alone. "It's less of a loss to the church if one dies rather than two or three."

The jeep had been several hours on the road when a score of police stopped us, training their weapons on us. They ordered us to get out, the bishop first. Pretending to be looking for weapons, they opened a little suitcase, but found only a Bible.

Actually they were looking for the bishop's homily for the village feast. They thought they might be able to find something that would compromise him. But no homily! The bishop never wrote out what he was going to say. He would prepare carefully, but then he would memorize only the general outline.

The policemen examined the Bible. "My only weapon," said the bishop. He said it fearlessly but gently, with even a note of respect for the policemen. Such a humble attitude exuded a certain majesty, and I thought of Jesus before Pilate. As a matter of fact it was the police who were getting jittery.

We were allowed to get back in the jeep and get going again.

Half an hour later we ran into another contingent of police, more aggressive than the first, seeing that the bishop had evidently decided to keep right on with the trip.

Back on the road.

Within sight of the village there was a final police roadblock. We go out. The men were forced to stand against a wall, their hands raised. Only the bishop was wearing a cassock, and the policemen lifted it, without showing any respect. The bishop didn't say a word. The villagers were already there, twenty yards away, and irritated at the way we were being treated.

An officer came up and said to the bishop: "Excuse me. We've learned of an assassination plot against you, so we had to take these security measures. I went to a Catholic high school. You will let me attend your Mass, won't you?"

"The word of the Lord is for you as for everyone. Besides, there are always plainclothes police when I celebrate Mass. But you know your uniform makes the *campesinos* edgy. Do be discreet."

The bishop entered the village on foot, surrounded by *campesinos,* while police blocked the side roads to keep other *campesinos* from joining us.

After Mass, everybody had a meal and the bishop sat in the middle of the court yard of the priest's house. We sat on the ground around him, where we could.

A villager began to strum his guitar. The atmosphere was simple and familiar. The bishop, too, was the son of a *campesino.*

Suddenly, a man stood up. We had already noticed him at Mass and during the meal. He was only twenty-eight, but he looked forty. Misery and famine had so ravaged his sun-tanned face.

His trousers were a patchwork of little bits of material, handsewn. His shirt was even scruffier. He was barefoot. He had put on his poor sandals only for the toughest of mountain trails.

No one here was well-to-do. But penury like this impressed everyone.

And yet, even more than his destitution, it was the man's eyes that captivated us, eyes brimming with light, as if they had already glimpsed a new world.

The man approached the bishop, coming to within two or three steps of him. He began to speak to him, but in such a way that we could all hear. The tone of his voice was brotherly, and ringing with faith, but with emotion, too, at the sight of the bishop of the poor.

"I come from across the border. I have been walking two days. I wanted to meet you. I am one of those they call guerillas. We hear your sermons every Sunday on the radio. We are glad that there is a bishop who understands the injustice we suffer. We know that your life is threatened on this account. But I say to you: *Go forward for the Lord is risen,* and no one can murder *your soul.*"

Visibly moved, the bishop embraced the *campesino* warmly.

Now other villagers and *campesinos* addressed the bishop, making little speeches and acting out little scenes, alternating with music and songs.

The bishop rose to speak.

"I thank you all, and especially our friend from across the border. It is because of what you say to me that I love coming to see you in the villages. I receive advice here that I never get in town. Down there they tell me, 'Be careful! Not too much talk of injustice!' Here, what I get are words of faith and encouragement that help me live the Gospel. The Lord is speaking to me through your mouths."

We left in the afternoon. We were stopped at the same spots as in the morning "to prevent an assassination."

Penny

24
All Together Now...
Europe

There we were, a little cramped, on the last bench at the back of the hall. I had twelve kids with me, ten to thirteen years old, all mentally handicapped to a greater or lesser degree. The bench was blocked by the wall on the right, so no one could get out that side, while I sat right on the left, on the middle aisle. That way things would be peaceful.

Here I wasn't the nurse any more. I had come simply to try to pray with my little band, at the eleven o'clock Mass, on this, the first Sunday after Easter. We embarked on this adventure only two or three times a year.

In front of us sat seventy boys and girls from the catechism classes, just as tightly squeezed onto the uncomfortable brown wooden benches as we were.

Only a few minutes before, as we waited to enter the hall, we had formed two quite distinct groups.

The catechism group, a little on the rowdy side, had stared at the handicapped kids, not knowing exactly how to react.

Our group of twelve had stuck close together, shyly, almost fearfully.

Now, on our back bench, nobody was looking at us anymore.

The hall with its off-white walls had nothing of a church
about it. The spring light made the most of the big windows on
the left, playing over the flowers on the very simple little altar
and making the altar cloth gleam. It illuminated the big letters
on paper pinned to the wall behind the altar: "Jesus lives!" All
around this proclamation of the Good News were drawings by
the kids.

The Mass began.

The atmosphere was relaxed, and nobody was too concerned about discipline. Everybody knew the songs. The priest
was a good teacher, and had a way of praying that kept
everybody's mind on the Mass.

The liturgy of the word went off without a hitch.

We came to the offertory. The kids struck up, "All my life
I will sing your name, O Lord."

That was when Marie-Claude got up.

We'd wedged her smack in the middle of the bench,
because she's the hardest to control. She's also the most
severely handicapped. She's ten years old, but can't hold a
pencil to draw and can't button up her clothes. She can
pronounce a few words, but doesn't speak in sentences.

Marie-Claude got up. She came over towards me, and got
into the middle aisle. When something gets into her head, it's
better to let her do it. Besides, what if she wanted to go to the
lavatory?

Wrong guess. She started along the aisle, till she was half
way up it.

The kids were still chanting, "All my life I will sing your
name," swinging into the refrain.

Marie-Claude stopped.

Slowly she lifted her arms and turned.

The kids were amazed. All eyes were glued on her.

And again the refrain: "All my life... "

Then came the real surprise. The eleven on our bench started clapping in time to the music, and trying their best to sing the refrain.

It was catching. The seventy others, in front of us, also began clapping in time with the verse they were singing with the priest.

Marie-Claude, her pretty, dark eyes now sparkling, was still dancing.

Her brown hair, straight, slightly tousled, without a parting and combed forward, almost reached her thick eyebrows. Her mouth, made for smiling, was half-open. She was a real southerner, suntanned, thin, petite, in those trousers that looked so terrific on her.

There was a holiday mood now. It was great, singing and clapping together. Handicapped or not, everybody was in on the act. This was something different! The least among us had demolished the impassible barrier.

Mini-prophet!

Marie-Claude stopped dancing.

Calm returned.

She moved quietly up to the altar and stopped, her arms stretched out in front of her.

The priest began the Eucharistic prayer and said the words of consecration.

Marie-Claude placed her hands on the altar.

The singing began again: "Jesus lives. He will come again. He is here." But no more clapping. Something had happened.

Marie-Claude returned to her place, dancing quietly but disturbing nobody.

The Mass came to an end. Everyone went out.

The two groups re-formed. Each stared at the other, with fear or embarrassment.

Back to normal!

Ian

25

Secrets of a Likeable
Good-for-Nothing

Asia

I've lived with Muslims for twenty years now, and I'm counting on ending my days in peace among them.

I have nothing to say that my neighbor couldn't tell you just as well. There's nothing extraordinary about my life.

But life's ordinariness is in itself very beautiful.

I'm a house-painter. I'm forty-five years old.

I don't know why, but the minute I get to the yard, my workmates hug me. They're from the mountain.

I'm like their personal dustbin. They tell me everything they've done day and night.

They send me to the corner café six, seven, eight times a day for tea. I'm the town pet.

I'm supposed to pray on the job, otherwise they tick me off.

When they see I can't take any more work, they tell me stories. They tell me how God is closer to me than my own heart.

They call me Bulbul — "Nightingale" in these parts. It's because I laugh at everything, even if sometimes I may be crying inside.

When I get tired of my pals and the neighborhood, I get on my motorbike. I set off to proclaim the kingdom of God pretty well all over the place with a smile. A hello for one, a meal with another, a kind word to a little old lady, an innocent wink at a pretty girl.

At night I fall asleep like a child.

When I can't sleep, I walk around town, and throw myself into the arms of a child or a beggar.

If I'm seeking the Lord, it's Him I find written all over their faces.

I don't care for big words about love. I just love the One who hides under the roof of the poorest of the poor ... or behind the bishop's desk.

Each day, then, reveals His splendor. And His face has never disappointed me.

For sure, He whispers to me — and others around here say the same thing — that I'm a likeable good-for-nothing and shan't have a statue in the Vatican.

Who cares? I'll still be the one to be dealt the Lord's last card: to be a child.

The One who ravished my heart has taken me by the hand. I follow him fearlessly. I know he'll respect my frailty.

Tom

26

Christmas Ball

Latin America

"Don't go! Every time there's a feast they kill each other there."

Is that what decided me to go? Whatever it was, I went. The village was a long way off, somewhere on the plain, with a single dirt road, a few little prefab one-storey houses, a chapel, an infirmary, and a school, all lost in foliage and fields where everything grows like a garden of paradise. The faces and customs make you think you're in Africa, but the language you hear is Spanish.

Christmas was coming. Nine days before Christmas, I got a score of young people together every evening and our singing rang joyously through the houses.

Each morning at about three-thirty the boys woke the village by ringing the car-wheel rim they used as a bell. This was the tradition here. Villagers started heading for the chapel, until there were a good many of them there.

At four a.m. we interrupted the carolling and gathered round for a Gospel reading. Then we reflected on it aloud. And before the cock crowed, we were on our way home.

The teenagers and I took it into our heads to go carolling in front of every house. We sang everything we knew. We hammered and scraped on anything we could beat time with. What a din!

Christmas looked as if it was going to be really nice. Some youngsters had practiced forming a living crèche, and they were going to act out the Christmas story, as it is told in the Gospel.

December 23. Clear the decks! Men whitewashed the chapel and women cleaned it. Young people brought flowers and hung up wreathes and palms.

All week long the women had helped each other to pound maize in order to make liquor. The cheese fritters were ready. Each family would present its own to the Christ Child at the midnight ceremony. Then everything would be shared out as a sign of unity.

December 24. Everything was ready for the loveliest Christmas ever.

But alas that evening tragedy was in the offing...

The liquor shops opened. Juke-box music from the edge of the village began to pierce the night air, and under the multicolored lights, dancing began.

Ten p.m. Some of the kids came looking for me. They had hoped the dance wouldn't start till the service was over.

Eleven p.m. Villagers started for the chapel.

The devil was on his way too. Some of the men had already drunk a lot and the two policemen were sloshed.

In the darkest corner of the village two brothers were fighting, daggers in their hands. There was so much shouting and screaming that we went over. One of the cops staggered up and clubbed one of the brothers over the head with his night stick. The man collapsed in a heap. Everyone was speechless. They carried the man to the infirmary.

The adults and I went back to the chapel, where we found the young people. There were between thirty and forty of us. A man spoke up, "Better put the service off till tomorrow. There won't be anybody else coming now."

So we sang a carol, said the Our Father, and prayed for the sins to be forgiven.

There would be no service but the dance would continue.

Everybody went home. I went back to the house of the family who were putting me up. I stretched out in my hammock behind the house, under the leaf roof, where the family slept. The dance music still sounded in my ears, though muffled.

12:30 a.m. I awoke with a start. That was a shot!

I rushed outside. Villagers were running towards the chapel. There, in front of the chapel door, were the two cops. One was on his feet, completely drunk. The other was lying in a pool of blood. His colleague had shot and killed him with his revolver. They carried the corpse to the infirmary.

I went back to my hammock. I was very frightened. Everything was dark. The dance was over. It was 2 a.m.

Lying in my hammock, I couldn't get to sleep. I thought about all those who were experiencing the joy of Christmas.

Through the tears running down my face I tried murmuring, whispering, "A Christmas of peace,a Christmas of love."

But the words stuck in my throat.

Mary

27

End of the Road?

Europe

It was about six a.m. I'd done nearly 200 miles in a little over four hours. The storm had been raging ever since I'd started. I knew from the radio in my cab that the hurricane was blowing at over 60 miles an hour, and driving an empty 38-tonner through it took everything I had. When I rolled through a village I'd drive over piles of broken tiles that littered the street. The fields were strewn with torn-off branches. I was in a hurry to get where I was to take on a 22-ton load. That'd give my trailer a bit of stability.

Suddenly my headlights left the road and lit up the trees and sky. Caught in a miniature tornado, the truck reared up, collapsed on its side and left the road. A long slide in a shower of sparks. The lights went out, a tremendous crash, the motor stalled, excruciating pain, and swirling dead leaves in the crushed cab. All over in a matter of seconds.

Then I realized to my great surprise that I was alive. But I was caught in the wreckage, unable to budge, and soaking in diesel fuel from my ruptured tank. My heart was beating, though, and I was still breathing.

I could hear cars and trucks going by, but no one stopped. The long wait began...

All through the lower part of my body I felt nothing except for a terrible pain spreading everywhere. The most varied and contradictory feelings jostled inside me, as if spurred on by pain and the approach of death.

Panic and despair gradually took over as I realized that if nobody had stopped in the last hour, there was no reason to believe that anyone would decide to do so at all.

So this was the end of the road for me. This was where the Beloved would come to meet me, in the howling of the gale! This was where I would go to the Lord, my body lacerated and in agony.

To prevent myself from panicking, I prayed out loud, words and phrases from the Our Father and the Hail Mary. What a comfort these prayers are when death is imminent!

A kind of peace came over me as I realized that what I had always seen as the normal end of my life as a truck driver was in fact taking place. But it's awfully hard to give it up minute by minute, in rhythm with the blood flowing from your wounds.

I broke down. Wracked by sobs, I wept for a long time. If I could only lose consciousness...

Once more I turned to God. The mystery of Gethsemane. "If it is possible, take this cup away from me. Yet not what I want, but what you want" (Matt 26:39).

Dying alone... without a friendly hand or a tender look to help one cross the threshold.

Entering into the mystery of the Cross. Give everything. Die consciously, so that everyone may go to heaven, especially the truck drivers who pass by without helping me.

Do for love what so many others do out of necessity, that had been one of the rules of my life. Now I told myself, that I must also be able to die for love, for all those who die only because they must.

I reached these heights by fits and starts, by little leaps of faith and courage. But I was only a man, bruised, in pain, abandoned, and I took refuge with our Mother: "Hail Mary, full of grace... pray for me now, at the hour of my death." I repeated these words over and over, right out loud. Peace once more settled in my heart.

The pain grew less intense. It was cold and exhaustion that were coming over me now. The gift had been made. Why did this heart have to go on beating?

Probably in order to feel more intensely how good it would have been, in the last hour, to have had a brother, a friend, for company. How I'd loved to tell him, "My cup runneth over," that our life has meaning, and that it is marvelous, that God has never disappointed me.

To depart without a gesture or some form of witness. To have to leave thinking of the question mark there'd be about my last moments, that was painful too.

I didn't have much strength left now. I concentrated on my favorite prayer: "I abandon myself into your hands... I am ready for all, I accept this death. Let only your will be done in me and in all your creatures..."

The end of the prayer was too hard. How difficult it was to get those words out, often as I had said them, with their burden of eternity, in this hour of truth: "I offer myself to you with all the love of my heart... for I love you... I place myself in your hands with *boundless* trust, because you are *my Father.*"

It must have been about eight a.m. for it had been about half an hour since a pale November morning had dawned. My horizon was twisted sheets of metal and a little piece of grey sky. Not even the smile of a daisy... Let it all come to an end!

A car slowed down and stopped. A door slammed. A voice shouted, "Anybody in there?"

Summoning all my strength, I shouted back, "Yes! Quick!" No answer. Nobody came. The door slammed and the car drove off. Had I been heard?

I had twenty more minutes of uncertainty before the firemen came, quickly followed by a doctor and two nurses.

Gerry

28

The Big Wooden Beads

Europe

The ambulance from the next town stopped in front of our door. Two men came in for our mother. They put her on a stretcher. Mother moved her hand, without being able to say a word, as they carried her down the three steps to the street. The door swung shut.

Suddenly, there we were, six children, in silence, completely abandoned. We stood looking at the empty bed with the straw sack.

This was in 1949, after the war. I was only thirteen.

I can still see the low ceiling and big beams of our one room. Two narrow windows with little panes shed a bit of light on the whitewashed walls.

On one side of the room was a bunk bed, with lath sides. We all slept there on the straw, the four girls below and our two boys above.

On the other side, more or less beneath the two windows, stood an old outdoor table. Its grey paint was peeling off, and you could see the color of the wood in places. On either side of the table was a bench for the children, and at the end was mother's stool. Between the table and the bunk bed was her camp bed.

The only decoration in the room was a rosary. It was a big one, a foot-and-a-half long, of big, rough, unpainted wooden beads. It hung from a nail parallel with the left-hand window. It had occupied this prominent position over the table for three years. Glasses and bottles filled with wild flowers had been placed on the window sill to honor it.

I still recall how this rosary came to be ours. We were part of a column of refugees, crammed into a covered cart with three other families. Our mother was sitting in the back, facing backward, her legs dangling, towing a baby carriage with her four-week-old baby in it. Our father had recently died.

While we stopped to rest the horses, another group of refugees came up, on foot. A conversation ensued and a man we didn't know gave our mother the rosary.

Once we had a roof over our heads, we formed the habit of reciting a decade of the rosary together, one Our Father and ten Hail Marys, every night before going to bed.

Mother would take down the rosary from its nail, sit on her stool and begin the prayer. Often this gave rise to laughter or tears, as each of us wanted to be the one to hold the rosary. The youngest, especially, thought it was just wonderful to be able to squeeze the big beads in his little fingers.

So there we were, lost for words. Mother was really gone.

We went out to pick some flowers to adorn the sill under the rosary. It was May, Mary's month.

Some of the women who lived in the same building, refugees like ourselves, brought us something to eat and made sure everything was all right.

Then we arranged the room for the night. We took off our aprons and washed, because we were barefoot. We had agreed that we'd only say our prayers after that.

We decided that each of us would have his or her "own" day to start the prayers in Mother's place. Then we climbed up onto the table to reach the rosary, each of us trying to get it first. We lowered the wick of our kerosene lamp.

Instead of sitting on the benches as usual, we knelt around the table on the rough floor. And we didn't say just the one decade but the whole rosary, five Our Fathers and fifty Hail Marys.

The flickering of the kerosene lamp let me cry without anyone seeing.

Then we sang all the songs that came into our heads.

The neighbors were thinking: "Their mother won't be back."

But a few weeks later she was back! We couldn't believe our eyes! Yet it was true. Mother was there!

Everything gradually returned to normal.

It was only a few days later that we confided to her the secret of the rosary. Looking very pale, she smiled at us from her bed and told us. "This time you asked God to make me well. He heard you. From now on, you must always thank and praise Him."

How often that phrase has come to mind!

"Thank and praise God." Our mother taught us that by the whole way she lived. She didn't have to use many words. The language of her beautiful eyes was enough.

Today, thirty-five years later, the big, rough wooden beads have turned all dark and shiny.

Jill

29

"Come and sit by me!"

Africa

The little station quivered with heat in the terrible summer sun.

The train had just pulled in, covered with dust. As usual it was packed. Many of the poorer passengers found places on the roofs of the cars and sometimes even on the engine. The conductor would never get that far.

Now there was a general rush of people travelling third class. As many passengers wriggled through the windows as climbed through the doors. The enormous amount of baggage most had with them complicated things a great deal. Mattresses, blankets, provisions, chickens, pigeons, were all stacked among the passengers.

I managed to make my way over obstacles of every kind, and found myself safe and sound on the train. I was happy not to have trod on too many feet, and even happier to have managed to set my own two down right next to each other in the central corridor. I tried getting as comfortable as I could, standing, wedged in among my neighbors and clinging to a seat, my packages stacked all around me.

The train set off.

There was plenty of entertainment, even for those with the thinnest purses. A nice boy made his way along the corridor with a bucket of water on his shoulder. Bottles of Coca Cola were cooling in it, at least when they had time enough to cool. Then a tray loaded with glasses of mint tea would emerge, balanced above our heads and held at arm's length.

A blind man asked for alms, after singing verses from the Koran. A peddler had souvenirs to sell, pants for your baby, a ballpoint pen for your brother and all sorts of plastic gadgets made in Hong Kong. A cigarette vendor would sell you just two cigarettes if you couldn't afford a whole pack.

It all made you forget, for a moment, the heat, the flies, the dust, and your legs that were beginning to feel like lead.

The train stopped. One swarm of passengers wanted to get off and another to get on, both at the same time.

The train set off again.

The whole length of the carriage, the baggage racks were filled with soldiers returning from leave. Bent double, their heads against the roof, they were merrily swinging their boots over the heads of those lucky enough to have a place to sit.

One of the soldiers had been staring at me for a long time. He had an open, very youthful face. I could see by his eyes that he was unhappy to see me standing, especially when the bucket of water or trays of tea went by.

Suddenly I could see he had had a bright idea. He stared at a young man in the seat just beneath his feet and engaged him in conversation. Perhaps they had known each other since the beginning of the journey, for the train had been under way eight hours already.

Now I heard him say, "Ali! I have something to tell you. Come and sit by me!"

Ali did not budge. Obviously he was more interested in his comfortable place on the seat than in the confidences of his friend on the luggage rack.

Suddenly the soldier's face lit up again. From his perch, he had seen the Coke vendor coming back.

Politely, he insisted, "Please, Ali, come and sit by me and we'll have a Coke together."

I didn't understand immediately. I had my mind on my legs, which were slowly growing numb and moreover I was constantly having to make myself smaller, without losing my balance, to allow passengers moving up and down the corridor to pass.

The soldier gave me an imperious look, inviting me to take Ali's place as soon as he got up, before anyone else could move into it. Suddenly I grasped the situation, when I saw the soldier's broad gesture of welcome, addressed to both of us, Ali and me.

"Three Cokes, please!" he boomed to the vendor, who was slowly drawing near.

Ali climbed up the back of his seat and squeezed in among the soldiers. I tumbled onto the bench in his place, in time to receive, first, a bottle which the soldier was offering me. The next he gave to Ali.

I could not find words to thank him, especially as he was all discrete again, seemingly absorbed in his conversation with Ali.

Barbara

30
"Staying with the cows"
Africa

The fresh, pre-dawn air hit me. Except for an impatient calf calling for its mother, all movement within the high thorn fence which kept out wild beasts, took place in silence. The women were milking the cows before the flies woke up. Slowly the herds gathered outside in front of the enclosure.

A fiery sun forced its way through the ominous clouds of the rainy season. It painted in unreal colors the trees that were scattered like islands in an ocean of steppe and brush.

The big enclosure was empty now. There remained only the long, low cow-manure huts with the rounded roofs. Built right up against the enclosure, all the way around, they provided shelter for a little group of families comprising a *boma*.

The herds ambled off, one after the other, each led by a young boy armed with a spear.

There was plenty of work this morning. A great event was to take place that day. With a few women we cleared the ground in front of our neighbors' hut. It was no small matter to move that mixture of cow manure and mud from inside the enclosure. Luckily, the sun got in on the act.

A good hundred meters away, some women suddenly intoned a traditional chant. Adorned with countless pearls and necklaces, they drew near in single file grouped by the *boma*. Their long robes, plain red, or with red patterns on a white background emphasized their height and dancing gait. Our *boma* was filled with song and color.

In front of our neighbors' hut, the final preparations were under way. We set up two four-legged stools. Our neighbor had put on her finest robe, and her wide blue necklace. Her husband was draped in a red blanket.

In a few moments, their names would be Mary and Joseph.

Members of this nomadic people had been baptized before. But the ceremony had always taken place outside the *boma*, and all neophytes had abandoned their traditional way of life.

Now, for the first time, a baptism would be celebrated within the *boma* itself, in front of the family hut, where each great step in life was celebrated: circumcision, initiation, transfer of authority from one generation to another. The man of the day would be seated on the four-legged stool belonging to the head of the family and passed down from father to son.

At about 1:00 p.m. we heard the sound of a car in the distance. The bishop was arriving.

In single file and still singing, the women made their way down the hillside to welcome the new arrivals. Standing in a row, they greeted them, offering their hands and momentarily crossing thumbs with them.

Now the ceremony could begin.

Mary and Joseph took their places on the two ancestral stools a few meters from where the bishop stood in front of their hut. The women remained standing, in a semicircle.

Mary held her newest baby on her lap, where her other child leaned against her from behind. She was quite peaceful and collected, and let not a single detail escape her notice.

It was she who had insisted the ceremony take place in the *boma,* "so that the others will understand." For years now, she had been putting traditional melodies to the Our Father and the other prayers sung by the congregation during Mass. Today, as usual, she sang the verses, and the other women took up the refrain. There were no musical instruments, and no very rhythmic melodies.

There was a kind of bustle. The men were returning from watering the cows. With dignity they entered the enclosure. Each of them greeted the guests, Mary and Joseph, and the whole assembly, again with the outstretched hand and the crossed thumbs.

The ceremony could continue. Now the men could play their part. Just as it had fallen to the women to sing the praises and prayers, so it was the men's place to bless. Just like the bishop, as was the custom, they sprinkled the two neophytes, and the whole assembly with milk.

The baptism was over.

The women brought out dried biscuits and tea. But time was short, for goats and sheep were on their way back and would have to be seen to.

At sunset the cows took their place once more in the center of the *boma.* A few children still played among them.

Everything grew still again. The only sound was that of muffled voices in the huts. A dog barked at a passing hyena.

Alone, Mary and Joseph were still sitting in front of their hut, in the moonlight. Until late in the night they would speak of their joy of being "three times more brother and sister" than before, and of having been baptized in front of, and for their other sisters and brothers.

Mary would add: "They will see now that one can be a Christian and stay with the cows. Only one's heart need change."

Rose

31

Just an Ordinary Day

Europe

The belt started up.

We just had time to get ready, adjust our white caps, check the height of the platform where we stood in our boots, and tie our long, white rubber aprons over our pale blue uniforms with white collars. And most of all, check our knives.

We were in the filleting section. Our shed must have been fifty yards long. At the far end a battery of machines worked unceasingly at torturing the fish: cutting them in half, extracting their backbones, skinning them and pounding the bones into meal. The noise was thunderous, and one had to wear earplugs.

In our section they were optional. There were glass partitions between us and that machinery, but at the other end of the hall the packing-machines took it upon themselves to contribute their own share of din.

Between these two machine sections stood us women, the "filleters." It's enough to make you scared, isn't it? And I can tell you our knives were sharp. That's essential if you want to work quickly and well. Otherwise, you'd go crazy.

117

Today cod fillets were on the move.

With my left hand I dumped my first fillet on the transparent plastic slab, which was lit from below. With my right hand I used the knife to take out the side bones, which went, as required, into the opening on my right. The fillet went into the opening on my left. The tail had still a little further to go on the belt.

A matter of a few seconds, and my first fillet was on its way. On to the next!

That's it! Right in the gob. My neighbor on my right, no more than a couple of feet away, had made an over-hasty gesture and I got a faceful of fish juice. Not very nice.

Something St. Thérèse of Lisieux thought up came to my mind. In the laundry, a sister had carelessly splashed her face with wash water. "I made every effort to desire a great deal of dirty water, and I actually acquired a taste for this new form of aspersion, and I promised myself another trip to this happy spot, where such treasures were to be had." Not a bad way of looking at it!

So my neighbor got a smile from me and I one from her. The racket of the machines and the speed at which we had to work made any other exchange out of the question.

In any case we weren't much given to talking at the factory, even during our seven-minute canteen breaks. There we were certainly comfortable, though, on upholstered benches with green plants all around.

Our language was more that of the eyes. There were about forty pairs of us, lined up on either side of four conveyors. Our eyes could say, more quickly and more eloquently than words: "Everything O.K.?" "You're getting on my nerves!" "Break's coming up!" "Keep going!"

This absence of words made inner silence easier. Prayer got a choice spot. The Lord was there, but without barging in. In me, in each of us.

I would keep trying to come back to Him. I would say a special prayer for my neighbor. I would take a quick look up and down the belts and commend everybody there to God — while watching to see that I cut the fish, not my fingers.

It's starting again! As it does nearly every day... My workmates are beginning to force the face. I'm not lazy but that sort of rhythm is killing.

I could understand them, though. We were paid, as a team, by the number of fillets cleaned. Therefore our pay depended on the speed of us all.

I grumbled a bit. After all, money isn't everything!

I stepped up my rate.

I started feeling tired.

At such times I like to keep saying what is called "the Jesus prayer." It doesn't take very much energy or concentration. I repeat over and over: "Jesus, Son of the living God, have mercy on us sinners."

Or else, I say to Him: "Lord, increase our faith." Or again: "I'm here for You."

Actually I'm happy in the midst of my fish, even if what I'm doing isn't all that charming.

In fact, everything seems so simple. I can pray while earning my "daily fish," and still have a chance to be friendly and attentive to others.

The clock indicated time for the break.

I was glad to have a breather.

Maggie

32
Perhaps One Day He'll Tell Me

Europe

In 1941, during World War II, I returned to my country after eighteen months as a prisoner-of-war. My work in insurance entailed a good deal of travel, especially to X., where I would stay in a hotel.

In that city I renewed my acquaintance with a girl, M., whom I had earlier known very well. We would meet several times a month, and our friendship turned into something deeper. We planned to get married. The eternal story, and up to this point, altogether normal.

Was it a premature decision, as I have so often been told? I think not, for at that time I was "going out" several times a week, and had had the opportunity of getting to know other girls.

During the years before the war I had attended church very little, probably because of the life I was leading. Having often bailed me out financially, despite the fact that I had an adequate salary, Father had no illusions about my life. Nor had imprisonment improved me a great deal.

You need to know that to understand that I was not prepared for what was going to happen.

It was in my hotel room that God gave me to understand that I was not to marry. It is difficult to enter into the details of an encounter of this sort with the divine will.

It was tooth and nail, and it went on for three months.

I shall not soon forget the nights the Lord made me spend on my knees in that hotel room, praying at the foot of my bed, asking Him why He was against this marriage. I would emerge at once broken and soothed.

I could not tell M. for I could not accept it myself, and neither would she.

After two or three attempts to break off the relationship, it was in another town that things came to a head. On my way back from work one day, feeling pretty low, I "happened" to go into a church. I do not know why, for I seldom attended church, even since God had shown Himself to me. Probably because I had not accepted His will.

As it happened, in this church, the priest was just turning toward the people to impart the benediction of the Blessed Sacrament. It was at once the knock-out blow and enlightenment.

It all happened in unspoken words and images that were not to be located in any particular faculty.

God gave me clearly to understand that I was to enter the religious life, but as a "civilian," living in the world, and sharing the life of the poor. He gave me two godparents, two saints of whom I had very vaguely heard, the Curate of Ars and Thérèse of Lisieux.

Now I had only to write to M. and return her letters and photos.

The religious life is a sort of "spiritual" marriage, and this is what the Lord had sought to make me understand, having to use extreme measures, because persuasion had not sufficed.

I must say in my own defence that I had never contemplated any life for myself but the married life. God is free to do as He pleases, and the more unpromising the material, the more clearly His initiative should be seen to be divine.

But nothing of the kind ensued. Almost everyone believed that I had suffered a stroke of madness as a result of a "disappointment in love." And I must say that appearances were entirely against me.

I received many letters begging me not to do anything foolish, urging me to "think it over," and assuring me that I would "get over it."

Meanwhile, there I was, "on the street," with no very clear marching orders, inasmuch as what was asked of me did not exist. Everyone in religious orders wore a habit. Worker priests had not yet been invented.

What I can say, however, is that no one could have induced me to change my mind and, on the other hand, I should not have remained a monk for more than six months had not God constrained me to do so.

God had called me, and imposed celibacy on me, which I hadn't asked for. Let him understand who can! But I no longer hold it against Him.

What am I to conclude from all this?

It seems to me that God used the so-called experimental method, perhaps overdoing it at times, but it made me say yes and accept the consequences of that acceptance before letting me know the reason why.

Perhaps, one day, He'll tell me why!

Simon

(The writer of these lines died as a monk, a night watchman, thirty-three years after the "great encounter.")

33
Socks or the Cinema?

North Africa

They found him one morning lying by his bike under a leaden August sky. Death must have come suddenly.

It was him, all right, in his usual blue work trousers, shirt, grey woolen cap, and orthopedic shoes.

We mourned him like a brother.

Every Friday morning, just before prayer at the mosque, he would come to see us. He didn't go to the mosque himself, even though he was a Muslim. His disease prevented it.

He had been struck by leprosy, and cruelly. Most of each foot, and all ten fingers, were gone. It was torture for him to walk.

Even his face was disfigured. But an extraordinary smile transfigured it. His clear, cheerful look purified whatever it touched.

Yet those same eyes had stared at leprosy face to face. At the most terrible moment of the disease our friend had tried to drown himself. "But even the sea didn't want me, and I was washed up on the beach."

We didn't know how old he was. But he had the maturity of those who have suffered a great deal.

He lived on Thirty-Seventh Street, barely a hundred meters from the milling crowds of the marketplace. It was a sloping street lined with little, one-storey, whitewashed earthen houses.

His own house stood out from the others: a creeper with pink blossoms ran along the flat roof and fell to the street, right along the shop, the only one on the street.

It wasn't much, that shop. Our friend would wear the stumps of his hands raw filling his customers' baskets with charcoal.

Once the street door was shut behind us we were in his little yard. You would have thought you had reached an oasis of calm. Two earthenware jars of water, a few rabbit hutches, a little garden, a bench, and, especially, our host's contagious smile. You almost forgot the peddler's cries, the blare of the transistors, and the squeaking of the carts.

We sat down on the bench and relaxed, and our friend confided in us.

"You see, hunger is a terrible thing. Once I had no work, and nothing to eat. At last I said to myself, 'I shall just have to start begging.' I had never learned how. I simply sat by someone's front door. I said to myself, 'The people in this house will hear me.' I tried to think what to call out. I said to myself, 'Come, come now!' I took in a breath to begin but what came out was not a call, but 'Oo, oo, oo!' for I began to weep aloud! So I left in a hurry. And I walked about in the night. And then, I saw a freshly baked bread that someone had forgotten on top of a little wall. I understood that God was watching over me."

One day he announced to us: "I have a guest. I don't know for how long. He has the same disease as I. I said to him, 'You don't know where to go? Come to my house!' He came. He cuts grass for sheep and sells it at the market. In the evening we share what he has earned.

"Yesterday he returned with three beautiful coins. He had found them on the pavement. 'What shall we do with them?' he asked. We thought about it. Then I said to him, 'It is true that you need socks. But this money, here, we haven't earned it. God has given it to us. Why don't we go to the cinema? One needs a change of scene sometimes.'

"So we went to the cinema, and we had a very nice evening."

Liza

34

A Clubbing and a Wedding

Latin America

Hesitantly Don Luis stirred his cooked oats. "We are sorry to have disturbed you."

"Things are not good in the village," added his wife. The feud is on again between the Vera and Velasquez families. This time it's about the road that crosses the Vera son's property. Once upon a time, they forgave each other, but no longer. No one has any hope now. We have stopped meeting."

The priest and I would come two or three times a year to spend four or five days in the Christian community of this little lost village. On this trip, despite our warm welcome at the hands of Don Luis' family, we immediately felt trouble in the air.

The story of this division was an old one. Two families had been disputing over a tract of grazing land. Tensions had mounted. Don Miguel Velásquez, head of one of the two families involved, had even been dealt a blow on the head with a club.

Later, with the slow development of the Christian community, the families had been reconciled. For three years the community had lived in a Golden Age. Money was contributed for the digging of wells. A volleyball court had been laid out. It had been decided to build a classroom. And all came together at regular intervals to hear the word of God.

This time, then, it was a road that had put a question mark over everything. Slander and bad feelings were rampant. The villagers were taking sides, and were even threatening each other with death, a revolver or machete in their hand.

We made some contacts. Some villagers did want a meeting after all. And so, this evening, here we were in the home of Don Alberto.

Everyone present, including the young, had something to say about the affair. I busied myself jotting everything down on a chalkboard. Gradually the pattern of village life of these last three months began to emerge.

"The projects are stagnating. Interest is gone."

We asked why.

"The Velásquez family think that they are better than us."

"When one side wants to forgive, the other doesn't."

Complete silence reigned for a moment throughout the room.

"We are divided."

We had reached the heart of the matter.

Together we became progressively aware that the name of this crisis was *sin*.

The moment had come to measure our lives against the word of God. We chose texts dealing with forgiveness. To our great surprise, they were the center of attention during the days which remained.

Evening by evening the dialogue advanced.

"We have succeeded in coming together. Let us try to find the reason why we have been hating one another, so that we can ask one another's forgiveness."

"We must forgive each other from the bottom of our hearts. Otherwise it's no good."

"And till death! We must also commit ourselves to working for the community, through concrete actions."

It was a step forward. Everyone had come to realize that *all*, not merely a few, had sinned against the community.

"If we have faith, God will help us. We cry out in prayer in our most difficult moments. Just as we need three meals a day, so we need God's word."

On that evening, the third that we had met, we made a decision, one unimaginable only a few days before. On the following day two members of the community would visit the Velásquez to propose that the next meeting be held in their home, as in times gone by. In the home of the Velásquez, who were the cause of the division!

The next day Don and Doña Velásquez were silent at first, on their guard. Then slowly their features relaxed. Their eyes met. Bright smiles spread across their faces. The miracle had taken place. The answer was yes!

And to mark their reincorporation into the community, the old couple announced that they desired to regularize their marriage, in a religious ceremony at the next meeting.

That was a wedding not soon forgotten!

By nightfall the flickering light of kerosene lanterns converged on the Velásquez home. From far off we heard the welcoming drumbeat, and the song of the flutes, so pure and so familiar. Our hosts had donned their Sunday best. Doña Velásquez had decorated the table with a few flowers and lighted candles.

On the very spot where the division had occurred, the Lord was about to gather us in the Eucharist. He would seal the unity of the community, and the unity of Doña and Don Velásquez.

After the wedding Mass, the celebration continued. The music started up again and we all sat down to a meal of maize, rice, guinea pig, and drinks. One or another of those present would tell a little story, or even offer a reflection:

"Today Doña Rosa and Don Miguel have become an example for us to follow."

"The community they have formed between themselves is a symbol of the community of our village."

The drum and flutes would accompany the dancers until late into the night.

Patricia

35

Pentecost at the Gallows

Central Africa

Daybreak, 6 a.m. A guard opened the prison gate to admit the priest. He led him across the prison yard to a windowless, twelve-foot-square cell, where only the open door let in any light. There the governor, the prosecutor, and a few others were awaiting the arrival of the man under sentence of death.

There came the sound of chains dragging over the concrete pavement of the yard.

The prisoner entered, escorted by two armed guards. The well-built man wore only tattered trousers. He was barefoot. A link of his chain had been soldered around each of his ankles.

He stopped, and faced the authorities. Everyone stood up. The prosecutor read a long indictment and recalled the murder and thefts committed by the prisoner, to demonstrate the justice of the death penalty to be meted out to him. He announced that the hour of execution was at hand.

Completely overwhelmed, the prisoner sought to speak, but was silenced. The authorities left. The prisoner sat down on a bench in the cell, flanked by the two guards.

A dialogue ensued between the prisoner and the priest.

"Are you baptized?" "I don't know. Perhaps, when I was a small child and very ill."

The priest continued his questioning, for he was unacquainted with the prisoner. The latter seemed to know nothing about the Christian faith. But his desire to become a Christian became so evident that the priest asked him, "Do you wish to be baptized?"

The prisoner's face relaxed and expressed a certain serenity. "Yes, I wish to be baptized."

The priest then put a small cloth bag on the only table in the room. It contained all the items necessary for the administration of the sacraments in an emergency. The baptism took place.

The bag still lay open on the table. The priest started to close it. But then he hesitated, looked up at the prisoner, and inquired, "Do you wish to make your First Communion?"

The man's "yes" was so poignant that all hesitation on the priest's part disappeared. He would celebrate Mass, wholly unusual as it would be under these circumstances.

The physical circumstances remained unchanged, but the atmosphere was transformed. Around the table, the prisoner, his two guards, and the few other persons there were now praying together. The condemned man made his first, and last, communion.

Meanwhile the approaches to the prison were growing very lively. That morning the radio had announced the public execution of the prisoner, whose exploits were known to one and all. Some two thousand people were pushing and shoving to get choice places at the very front.

The gallows had been erected on rough ground by the side of the prison. A microphone stood in front of it, in case the prisoner would have some last words to say.

Suddenly... a deathly silence.

The prisoner, accompanied by his guards, came out of the prison and made his way towards the gallows. His chains had been removed. All eyes followed him.

The microphone was offered. He accepted.

First he confessed his sins to the crowd and acknowledged the justice of his punishment.

Then he continued.

"If anyone of you has been jealous of me on account of my wealth, my fine clothes, my life of pleasure, look on my poor, hanging body and see the wages of my sin.

"Let me be an example to you, to abandon the path of evil, and follow the path of good. To rob or to kill one's neighbor is a very bad thing to do.

"And you, brothers and sisters of my family, you also, my friends and acquaintances, don't weep over my brutal but well-deserved death. In any case, I should have had to die one day in one way or another.

"I beg the Christians among you to pray that my soul may not perish with my body. Some of you are casting stones at me. Others mock me. But before God, at this moment, I am full of repentance. And I have just received Him into my heart.

"One of my mates is still in prison. He is being held unjustly. The crime of which he is accused was mine alone. I beg for his release."

The prisoner spoke for quite a time, his voice filled with assurance.

Then, with a firm step, he mounted the platform on which the gallows stood. He offered his feet to be bound.

For more than fifteen endless minutes he would swing, without a gesture, until at last he expired.

Mike

36

A Taxi to the Grand Hotel?

Southern Europe

Nine p.m. The neighborhood hadn't changed much since that great day four months earlier. I recognized an occasional barrack among the grey, uniform pairs lined up unimaginatively, in parallel rows.

Four months ago, the "shame of the city," a gypsy slum on the beach, had been eliminated.

In a single day, its inhabitants had all been transported to this neighborhood of prefab barracks. I'd left my regular gypsy group to lend a hand, and so I'd become acquainted with quite a number of families.

It was Christmas Eve. Was that why the nightly campfires, burning before practically every barrack, seemed to sparkle in the night with a livelier glow? They crackled joyfully, throwing showers of sparks.

The campfire is more or less the heart of a gypsy group. They cook there, meet each other and run over the events of the day, sitting on old chairs, boxes or the ground. The glow of the fire casts a reddish hue on their bronzed faces. The flames make earrings and bracelets gleam, and play on the bright-colored neckerchiefs and dresses.

The kids rush everywhere, jostling everyone. They are the little kings.

On this particular evening, the vigil would last till midnight, as custom demanded. As I knew several groups there, I moved from one to another.

"Over here!" I sat near a fire round which a few families were gathered. They offered me wine.

Having exchanged our news, I suggested, "Shall we talk about Christmas?" This was natural and easy for me, as I was to a certain extent one of them.

I read a short passage from St. Luke where Joseph and Mary journey to Bethlehem and there's no room for them in the inn.

Then I would comment:

> "They have to go and register at the town hall, just the way you have to go back to the town where you're registered every time you have a new baby, even if you are far off at the time, busy picking fruit. How often have you not found yourselves travelling for an administrative formality? Or waiting in line? And as you go by, what do people do? They shut their doors."

All of my friends relived intensely the mystery of the birth of Jesus in poverty. It was their own mystery. When the poor are despised, God is despised.

A guitar resounded in the night. It was a typical song of the region about Joseph and Mary on the road. Oh, the beautiful songs they have there! They are so unforced, so emotional.

A man asked a question and I answered. The dialogue had the same tone as the ordinary evening conversation.

Alas, the vigil was over, too quickly.

The next day, Christmas day, I returned to the neighborhood to call on various gypsies whom I hadn't been able to meet the previous evening.

About ten young people were dancing in a cul de sac, between two pairs of barracks. The whole atmosphere was festive, from the rhythm of a guitar, to the well-combed curly hair, the boys' carefully pressed trousers, some of the girls' long flowery dresses. And wine added to the fun.

There came a pause. Time to catch your breath and have a drink.

As one or another of them recognized me, they came over to talk about last night's discussion.

A sharp-featured young man stared at me for a long time with his intelligent eyes. Then he said to me:

"Last night in our group I understood what you were saying. I was about to go to the bar, but I felt I'd rather stay and listen to you. What you said was true, and I thought it was great. You can tell us that stuff with no trouble. Because we're poor, we know what poverty and contempt mean.

"But now we're going to take a taxi, at my expense, to the Grand Hotel. I want to see if you have the nerve to say the same things to the rich. They're the ones who need a change of heart!" He said it in a clear, confident voice, and without a shadow of aggression. He wanted me to lay my cards on the table.

I was really caught short. At first I was speechless, dumb. I had thought of every possible thing they could ask me but this.

Clumsily, I answered, "I live with you. I want to stay with you."

Perhaps I was just afraid? Afraid of making a fool of myself at the Grand Hotel?

Garry

37

No Parking

Southern Europe

I'm forty, and except for my bad teeth, in good health. I've a good pair of sandals, and my pack is well stocked. I'm following a road which winds gently upwards to the mountaintop, with nothing but blue sky and a fairy-tale landscape below.

A few cars break the winter silence of sleeping nature. The few pedestrians I meet only accentuate my tramp's solitude and peace.

It's February, but I don't need a sweater. If the weather turns mild and I have a little money to buy a meal, my cup of happiness is full.

Winter does have its disadvantages, though, especially at night, when there's nobody to play cards with and no light left to read a book by.

I've been on the road six months now without finding a decent job. I'm not a fanatic for work, but I never got used to living without working. If we've got arms and legs they must be for something!

I don't complain, though. Until now I've always been able to make enough to live on. And, thank God, I'm easy to satisfy and happy with little.

While walking, I wonder what the next village will be like. Will I be able to find a corner to sleep in? Will the church be open? Will they have a drinking tap? Will they have any bread? I always ask myself these questions.

It's going to be cold tonight. The village isn't much farther now, but I'd rather sleep in a broad ravine planted with orange trees. I can light a fire there without being noticed.

I try to pray sometimes just to kill time. But the fantastic shapes of the flames constantly distract me. It's just impossible to concentrate on anything.

The temptation to look on my life as absurd hovers over me like a vulture over its prey.

If anyone were to come across me here, they would never guess how uprooted I feel.

And if they asked me, "Who are you? What are you doing? Where are you going?" the only thing I'd be able to say is, "I'm looking for God on the roads down here."

For me, everything begins again each time with a very simple gesture, repeated many times in my life: I drop everything and hit the road. Without setting myself a clear aim and taking only what's strictly necessary — a change of clothes, a sleeping bag, a pocket Bible.

This simple act takes a lot out of me. It's like a leap into the void. But once I've done it, everything is possible.

I feel close to St. Benedict Joseph Labre, the obscure tramp who passed like a shadow through the world. He was obsessed by one thing only: to live for God alone.

I've been on these roads for twenty years. My real adventure is an inner one. My only goal in life is still God.

Benedict Labre starved to death in Rome, while still a young man. A strange way to look for God! Surely there were other ways.

The important thing is not to stop along the way.

Bobby

38

The Parcel

North Africa

A whole day wasted in this little town I'd never seen before. No way of getting my visa. And tomorrow it would be the same wretched thing all over again.

A very "spiritual" reaction drove me to drown my anger and confusion in a café. A pleasant little Arab tune seemed to entice the flies to the place. The customers looked me up and down. I was neither an Arab nor a local.

I looked for a place and sat down opposite a guy who didn't look in any better shape than I was.

I dumped all my troubles on him. Ahmed did the same with me. He was out of a job and afraid to go home and tell his wife, once again, that he hadn't found anything.

We sipped quite a few glasses together.

"Where are you going to spend the night?"

"Haven't the faintest."

"Come to my place!"

He took me to a neighboring suburb. On a heap of rubbish was a little shack. This was it. Ahmed opened the rickety door to the single room inside. There was no furniture at all.

Fourteen pairs of mistrustful eyes mowed me down like machine guns. There were the parents-in-law, Ahmed's wife and... eleven kids.

We sat cross-legged on the floor. Ahmed introduced me and the looks gradually changed. They changed so much that the only memory which will remain is one of inexpressible sweetness. I felt welcomed, loved. Ahmed's wife hesitated, then withdrew the veil that had hidden her face — a mark of trust.

After quite a long absence she returned with a mountain of rice on a copper plate, doubtless their only valuable possession.

The rice quickly disappeared and we kept chatting, about everything and nothing. Glasses of tea kept us awake. Well into the night we all stretched out to sleep.

A rooster woke me. It was time to go. As we said goodbye, I promised to stop by again before catching the bus, for we knew we'd never see one another again.

Another day of trying to get a visa. Failure like yesterday. To hell with it! I'd take the bus that night, visa or no visa. I hurried over to thank my hosts.

They were expecting me. Everything happened quickly. When the moment came to say goodbye, they handed me a parcel, without saying anything, so rapidly that I almost didn't notice. Everything seemed to happen so naturally.

The bus was jam-packed and I barged my way onto it. I found a seat at the back and wedged myself in among my things.

Ah, yes. The parcel. I opened it discreetly, as my neighbors were looking at me. Actually my mind was still mostly on my visa.

Suddenly my eyes filled with tears. I was going to cry, for a good half hour, completely overwhelmed by what I had just found in the parcel. I didn't care now what the other passengers might think.

There in my lap was the copper plate from which we'd eaten the rice. And a little rubber camel... the kids' only toy.

Dan

39
A Tramp's Nostalgia

Southern Europe

The city was marvelous in winter.

I spent a few hours on the edge of the pavement opposite the cinema posters on Avenida Grande. For a tramp this was the best spot in the city center, for it was there that the morning sun reached first. The cold was easier to bear then.

Any moment now my buddy would come along with his cartons of cigarettes. He'd settled down beside me to carry on his little business. We'd been meeting there for several days now. He'd told me practically the whole story of his life. But I still didn't know his name!

Later that morning the beggar would be along, in his old overcoat and his scarf wrapped around his head. He took in more money than the cigarette vendor, but this didn't stop the vendor from looking down his nose at someone who would stoop to begging for a living.

There wasn't much doing. The morning began to drag, and we had a chance to talk. The cigarette vendor told me about a place where meals were cheaper than anywhere else in town. The beggar confided to me that you could take in quite a bit at the door of a certain church after the seven o'clock Mass.

Tomorrow or the next day we would part company, the cigarette vendor, the beggar, and I. Would we ever meet again? A change in the wind, and the tramp is gone, missed by nobody.

On the road again...

As I approached the city of X., I began to recall the faces. It was already two years since I'd stopped in on my friends there. Only their Christmas card had let me know that they were still there, and that their community-life project in a poor migrant neighborhood was still on its feet.

The door was open when I arrived. Two years is quite a while! Nothing had changed, though. I'm not much of a talker, but in no time the bonds of friendship were renewed. I was "at home" once more.

"How long are you here for?"

"Say, we're going to need you for some repair work!"

"Stay till St. Joseph's Day, at least. That's my feast!"

It was wonderful to be so well received. It's so nice to sit around a table, talking and playing cards.

Thank God friendship's free. And it's actually better and more sincere when you have nothing to give but yourself.

I may as well admit, I don't have the courage to say goodbye. Perhaps I'd slip away quietly, like a loner before daybreak.

My friends are my roots. I have to return to them from time to time, for it's thanks to them that I can stand frequent solitude.

It wasn't easy to learn I needed them. The untamable little loner that lives in me believed for a long time that he could live his adventure alone.

A tramp's greatest privation is not having anyone nearby to love. I have learned this by frequent cruel experience. This is the only poverty I cannot accept.

For sure, when I'm working here or there I feel useful. No one looks down on me. But with the present unemployment, I have to go miles all by myself without pals to work or celebrate with.

I try hard to treat every person I meet as a brother or a sister. But that's pure utopia. I notice the doubtful looks cast at me all right, the gestures of contempt or mistrust. With the years you grow wilder, and the hurts make your heart harder.

Joy and sadness succeed each other from encounter to encounter. And I go on my way, nostalgic for a universal community.

Even if it seems ever to recede with the horizon...

Bert

40
The Party at Doña Rosita's
Latin America

"Oh, Mama, walk ahead of me! They mustn't see you're my mother!"

This thirteen-year-old girl had been found a place by her mother in a fancy private school. It would never do for her classmates to discover that her mother lived in our slum!

"Blessed are the poor." At times it's hard to believe that. One dreams of imitating the rich, and of being able to forget, if only for one evening, the stigma that one carries.

The little scene reminded me of a family in our slum. They wanted to celebrate their daughter's fifteenth birthday in the way that the rich do. Only two or three families in our neighborhood could have afforded the luxury.

So they borrowed the home of a rather better-off friend, far from the slum. The invitation hinted that long dresses would be appropriate for the girls and dinner jackets for the boys. That immediately reduced the number of those who could afford to come. Most of them would be coming from one slum or another, but there was a kind of understanding among them all that certain others would not be coming, so that the "tone" of the celebration would not be lowered.

The guests began arriving about seven. Each was dressed as best as could be managed. I found it difficult to recognize this or that person with whom I rubbed shoulders every day. How many days' pay for these dresses, which would be worn only for a day! And did all that kinky hair really have to be straightened like a white person's? Several guests were inclined to pay more attention to the handsome toilettes than to the person underneath.

The guests sat down on the few chairs or else remained standing. Some, in a rather affected fashion, tried to play a role. But the basic spontaneity of the slum came to the fore here and there: friendly winks would fly from one table to another, while out in the garden, behind the house, pleasant little groups were talking, joking, or playing with squabbling little urchins.

Otherwise, though, it was hard to know what to do or say. The top hits, belting out of the stereo, discouraged conversation. All we could do was drink and watch the dancers. It was a colossal bore. You dreamed. You felt as if you were at the cinema.

Midnight came, and the customary ritual could at last be performed. In came the elaborately sculptured birthday cake, covered with pink and blue icing and lit with candles. The honor of cutting it fell, of course, to the girl who was fifteen today.

Once they had eaten their piece of cake, the sensible guests took their leave.

Nothing was left but debts, and an after-taste of sadness.

On the other hand, when Doña Rosita gave a party in the slum, you would think you were on another planet. Talk about fun!

Doña Rosita was not the poorest person in the neighborhood. But, on principle and by temperament, she never let money stick to her fingers when it was question of sharing, especially on Christmas Eve. Whether there were ten, twenty, or thirty of us, her door was open.

We arrived at night, after Mass. Everyone was singing, beating on drums, or strumming one or another stringed instrument. What a racket! The room was packed. You sat where you could, either on the floor or squeezed with several other guests into one of the three armchairs. Some squatted outdoors, each group as noisy as the next. Then the cold drinks went around, as it was the height of summer. Glasses would be rinsed, refilled, and passed from hand to hand to other thirsty guests.

Bursts of laughter echoed from the kitchen, where Doña Rosita was bent over a huge pot, a ladle in one hand and a bowl in the other. We all made our way to the kitchen, by turns, to enjoy her delicious vegetable soup.

But the pièce de résistance was her renowned corn pasta, stuffed with 36 different delicacies and folded in a banana leaf. Without it Christmas wouldn't be Christmas!

A shadow appeared in the doorway. Don Simon, father of a large family, an old man with very dark skin, had arrived. He wore his hat crammed low over his kinky hair. His big moustache and heavy eyebrows lent a finishing touch to his unique appearance. He looked around and smiled. Don Simon was a superb guitarist, and we adored his voice. We all clapped to get him to play. Silence fell.

His huge workman's hands began to caress the guitar with extraordinary agility. Everyone was enthralled by his voice. Sometimes he would hesitate, and stop. A blank in his memory. Lack of practice. And then there would be more applause and cheers to encourage him to play on.

Heat, sleep, worries, and struggle were all forgotten. The magic of Christmas had blended us all into one family.

Don Simon took a well-deserved breather. A young man of eighteen recited some of his own verse. In his words, his mimicry, his voice and his look, emotion, humor, pungency, and sometimes seriousness, appeared in turn.

There was a great burst of laughter. It was the inevitable little Ana, our clown. All she had to do was appear and everyone would be roaring with laughter. With a knack and flair which were priceless she would mimic anybody you wanted.

On the party rollicked, far into the night. Some of the guests would still be there at dawn, sitting out of doors, busy with song or discussion.

"Blessed are the poor." At Doña Rosita's party, that Christmas Eve, I believed it.

Pauline

41

All the Way to the End of the Caravan

Southern Europe

The rich aroma of coffee wafted through Genia's and Nito's caravan. I was sitting there, with a few friends, all warm and cozy. Rain fell noisily on the roof. Muffled sounds could be heard from outside, a motor starting up, a mother chasing after one of her kids.

The boys must have been dawdling somewhere with their gang. The three older girls were doing the dishes and tidying up. The little ones were playing, quietly for a change, on the floor and sofas.

Genia, the mother, was breastfeeding her year-old baby. "Children bring joy," she said. When you have twelve, to say that means something!

Nito, her husband, was a short, skinny little man, nervous and reticent. He had a drooping moustache and his look was vivacious, self-assured, and somewhat mocking.

He had been in a car accident, and had spent the whole summer lying in a plaster cast that went all the way from his

155

chest to the toes of one of his feet. Even one of his arms was immobilized. Little by little, though, he had cut away the pieces of his "casing" wherever they became too bothersome. Leaning on his free leg, he was now practicing moving round a bit.

A neighbor or relative was always on hand to help him eat, move him, or give him a good scratch!

The baby finished feeding, and his mother handed him over to his ten-year-old sister.

One was never bored with Genia. Small and thin herself, she wore her dyed blonde hair tied back at the neck. She loved to tell stories and laugh. With her raucous voice, she was better than an actress. She could pull out all the stops for the occasion: her sparkling eyes, her heavily painted face, her big, shaking earrings and her pathetic gestures. With the help of a local sweet wine, it became high art.

Nito, at one end of the caravan, was fiddling with his radio, looking for his favorite music, and not paying a great deal of attention to the story his wife was telling. It was "old stuff" as far as he was concerned.

One of the kids acted up. Genia delivered one of her interminable broadsides, which sound like a thunderclap — only the lightning never fell.

"Now where was I?" she said. "Oh yes, the other night we were already in bed. Nito was still in the same place as in the daytime, at the end of the caravan. I was in bed with the baby at the other end, between the bunk beds. You know, it's hard enough for Nito to sleep as it is. So if the baby starts crying, that's it for him. No more sleep.

"I couldn't get to sleep myself. I was worried. We've got fourteen mouths to feed, and with Nito not working it's hard on the wallet.

"Well, you know what happened? I saw my Nito trying to get up. I was frightened, thinking he was going to fall. But no, he made it, upright, crabwise, on his good leg. I pretended to be asleep."

Genia talked, declaimed, and I could see it all as if I'd been there. Nito hung on to the shelving that went practically the whole length of the caravan, and moved himself along in little hops, sideways. By the light of a small electric lamp, left burning all night, he just managed to miss the children sleeping on the floor. It was a miracle that his leg cast didn't scratch one or the other of them.

"There he was, in the middle of the caravan. What was he trying to do, at this time of night? He continued his way across toward the bunk beds.

"I kept pretending I was asleep. He came up to where I was. He grabbed onto the bed, and leaned down. How, I don't know. And you know what he did? He kissed the baby and caressed me. Just like that! Without wanting to wake me up.

"I didn't move a muscle. I kept pretending to be asleep.

"He went back as he'd come.

"Well, that was the end of my money worries. All I could think of was how lucky I was. If I hadn't met my Nito, I'm sure I'd have ended up streetwalking."

And she turned to Nito. "Once you're out of that cast we'll have another kid! And don't worry, we'll get along fine!"

And she burst out laughing.

Fred

42

The Shepherd at the Stable Door

India

Our dirt road, shaded by great trees, looked as it did every day, even though today was Christmas. We were the only Christians in this little Hindu village.

To share the joy of Christmas with the other villagers we had made a crèche. We had put it in our front room, and had left the door open. This way, anyone who wanted could come and see it and pay us a visit.

Villagers had been dropping in pretty much all day. Quite a number of little kids came by with their parents. In fact, whole groups of boys and girls came in and sat down. Adults came by too, but they didn't have time to sit down because of the pressure of work.

Everyone who came was enthralled by the crèche.

It looked like the poorest of poor huts, a sort of stable, like the ones in the village. The roof and walls were of rice straw, golden yellow.

The painted statuettes were four to six inches high, and you would have thought that they were real villagers. The

Christ Child, wrapped in a piece of white cloth, looked up at you
and stretched out his arms as if in welcome. Mary, in a sari and
blouse, was kneeling on the Child's left. Joseph, girded with a
long white cloth and wearing a shirt, was standing.

Around the Child were many other statuettes. Not far from
the crèche a woman was pounding rice. Others, outside the
stable, were selling bananas, rice and coconuts. A very
swarthy man robed in white was walking along carrying a bag
of rice. There were also a few shepherds. And children, poked
in among the sheep to see Baby Jesus.

A little lamp burned in front of the crèche.

To one side, a big picture book told the story of Jesus' life,
from birth to resurrection.

The boys and girls wanted to know more about him. One
of them picked up the book and began to read aloud. The
others listened in wonder. They asked us lots of questions. As
for the adults, they spoke to one another in undertones.

As was customary for a festival day, we shared sweets and
pancakes.

As evening was falling, my friend the old cobbler appeared
in the doorway, with his crown of white hair. He looked as he
did every day, wearing a white loin cloth but no shirt. No
sandals either, unlike the other villagers. He was the poorest
person I had seen in the village.

He came here regularly from a neighboring village. In ours
he had no roof of his own. He would stay two or three days,
sleeping in the stable where he worked. He spent the days
taking the cows to pasture, cleaning out the stable, or carrying bundles of rice stalks. He received no wages, but only
something to eat.

He was a person of great kindness, and completely
humble. He spoke little, slowly, and in a very soft tone. He
never complained.

Everyone avoided him for he was a cobbler.

According to tradition, he was unclean, "untouchable," for
he worked with cowhide.

I had met him for the first time not long before Christmas. Shivering with cold, he was standing outside on a very windy day. I invited him in and presented him with a blanket from one of our beds.

This was the first time he had set foot in a house in our village. And everybody let him know that he was not to do so again.

There he was, then, at our door.

I beckoned to him to come in, despite the protestations and expressions of disgust on the part of the boys and girls sitting in front of the crèche.

I hadn't thought of him particularly this Christmas Day. I couldn't imagine what had brought him to our door. Had he guessed that we were Christians because we lived a little differently? At any rate, I don't think any of the villagers would have mentioned anything to him about Christmas.

The poor old cobbler came through the door. He moved toward the crèche. He fell on his knees, hands joined, as if in deep prayer.

Imagine my astonishment, and that of our guests, when we saw him make the sign of the cross.

Someone whispered to me that he was a Christian.

I had had no idea.

He would not have known that it was Christmas, had he not been passing by and seen that stable.

He went away, to sleep on his own.

John

43

"Even if my child should die"

North Africa

Four young European tourists were there at the entrance to the little hospital, with a tight group of neighbors and relatives. A man was carrying a six-year-old boy in his arms. The little one was unconscious, his face all covered in blood. Anxiety was written on everyone's face.

The child and his mother were admitted to the unit where I worked, and everything necessary was done.

The accident had occurred that afternoon in a little village fifteen kilometers away. Little Mohammed had darted out from behind a parked bus, and the tourists' car had sent him flying five meters back up along the side of the road.

Night had fallen when they came back for news. The group was admitted to the unit. I opened an outside door and led the tourists into the court. I was able to give them reassurance. The doctor's diagnosis and the X-rays were encouraging.

I heard the door open again. A woman came up to us and stopped by me. It was Mohammed's mother.

In an astonishingly self-confident voice, she said to me in
Arabic: "Tell them that they can rest assured. Nothing happens
but by God's will. I shall not lodge any charge against them.
Even if my child should die."

She pronounced each word with an unusual intensity, like
a heartfelt cry. The deep silence of the night served only to
amplify its significance. I was bowled over.

I spent the evening in the home of a woman who was my
neighbor. We watched a beautiful TV film, one typical of that
country. In a village a young man has been murdered. His
mother swears vengeance. Disguised as an old man returning
from a pilgrimage to Mecca, she goes to the assassin's village.
There, one day, the right occasion presents itself. The "old
pilgrim" has a meal with the murderer. The murderer, taking
his victim's mother into his confidence, finally admits to the
crime. The mother gets up, tears off her pilgrim disguise, pulls
out a dagger, and deals the murderer a mortal blow. Then she
calmly makes off to surrender to the police. The film was over.

My friend was simply glued to the screen. She felt intensely
for the heroine, admiring her courage, her wiliness, her
success. It wouldn't have taken much for her to plunge the
dagger in at the same time as the actress.

"Eye for an eye, tooth for a tooth." Here in the countryside,
that was the norm. Especially for a mother when it concerned
her children.

The film, and my friend's reactions to it, made me
appreciate the unusual, extraordinary nature of Mohammed's
mother's forgiveness.

"I shall not lodge any charge against them. Even if my child
should die."

Some time later I heard something else about Mohammed's
mother, and I was even more surprised. In that same hospital,
she had already lost a child, barely two years before.

The father had been sent for, and entrusted with the little
corpse. Beside himself with grief he had taken it home in a

basket. Unable to bring himself to break the news to his wife, he had hung the basket on a tree in the yard.

The mother, intrigued, had opened it...

The shock had been too great. It had taken her over a year to recover.

Anne

44

My Favorite Places to Pray

Europe

In big western cities work, often done alone with a machine, forms one part of a person's life; after which we disperse and shut ourselves up at home.

It is like standing on a river bank, with humanity streaming by at your feet but without seeing any friends there, without actually encountering anyone. It's a solitary life. Meetings happen by chance, or on the margin of daily living.

This is what I have come to look for here, by renting a little room in order to experience the human loneliness that is the lot of so many in the big cities.

In this lonely room I have had asthma attacks to the limit of what I could bear. I have discovered what it is like to suffer and die alone, as so many do.

You can read a great deal in the faces of the crowds in big cities. These, with daily events and the people you meet, make up the whole book of life.

For a number of weeks now, I have felt a new friendliness for these crowds.

As I was looking at these faces, jammed together in the subway, passing from the light of the stations into the darkness of the tunnels — in a little replica of life — the Lord let me know that this was where my brothers were, and that I was one of them, that I had not parachuted in among them as a stranger, but had been chosen from among them as an intermediary, to speak in their name.

I was to discover all of a sudden the meaning of the word "brother." To observe faces and quickly try to understand them, to get to know their nationality and their character, to ask for each one what seemed necessary to him or her, and to unite them to their Father, and their God.

I have only two free evenings a week but each time it means a new encounter. A girl at her wit's end, a woman just out of the hospital, hardly able to walk, a young woman on the verge of prostitution.

God is there with them, in these passages, in these underground cars, on the sidewalks.

The street and the subway are still my favorite places for praying.

God has always come to me in the most ordinary places.

There are also the old churches. I've always loved to pray in churches. Perhaps because it's there that God called me to the religious life.

In a church I discover my place as a link in the human chain, which has grown to be long in the other world and which trails down to the earth.

It's very difficult not to see yourself as part of humanity in this great city, for in twenty-four hours you rub shoulders with a representative of every country in the world. You feel very strongly the weight of the sufferings and the events you come across. This produces a kind of weariness.

I spend two afternoons a week in a church if I can. I stay for three or four hours, resting in God.

My work as a night watchman also affords me thirty-six consecutive hours of solitude and absolute silence on weekends.

For thirty years now, I've tried to pray as continuously as possible because of my need to lean on God.

I have difficulty fixing my attention on a book, and my reading consists in looking at Bible passages or very short texts. I think my attention is easily enough attracted by all life's and God's mysteries.

I know what it is to spend nights in meditation before God, unable to sleep because of asthma attacks. I substitute silence for my vanished sleep. My tiny garret has become a regular hermitage. It looks out on all the roofs, and I have the pigeons for my companions.

Simon

45

Death of a Night Watchman

Europe

It was five-thirty on a February morning.

A cleaning lady entered the large office building and spoke as usual with the night watchman who had let her in.

Seven-forty.

A painter came to the same door, to start the day's work. It was locked. Puzzled, he headed for the other building in the same complex.

There, outside, at the foot of the steps, he found the lifeless body of the night watchman. He was lying on his back, a very long and thin form, with his feet on the second step and his head on the ground.

It looked as if he had started up the steps. The palm of one hand had scratches on it, as if he had grasped at the concrete wall along the steps. The doctor thought he had suffered a heart attack.

Someone had just died, alone, on the verge of retirement. He had died like so many others found dead, one fine morning, their secret gone with them.

The watchman, too, had very nearly gone off without telling his secret.

But just three days before his death, in his tiny rented room, he had finished a very long, very personal letter to his brother. This was quite contrary to his habits, his temperament and to the silence he had kept about his life, that of a convert turned monk.

The last sentence of the letter was astonishing.

"I've been hoping the Lord won't leave me on earth much longer since I've been asking Him to take me. I'm sure one is more useful gone than here if that's His will."

Three days before his death.

Death and the night watchman were old acquaintances. You need only read passages from his last three letters.

"When you've suffered from asthma all your life, and faced death many times, you've studied the question from every angle.

"But death is like love. It's not real till it has a particular face. For months now, it has appeared to me in one form: death by suffocation.

"You fear what you thought you'd left behind long ago. You always want to say to God, 'Anything but that…'

"For months I've been crossing an inner desert where everything becomes heavy. What keeps me going is a kind of routine loyalty to a friend who seems to have disappeared. Deep down inside I say yes, but as a man in some way diminished because I no longer feel, or see, or believe.

"These waves of desert inside me sometimes enable a better understanding of how God teaches us.

"It's what happens in a marriage. At first a couple needs to feel close to each other, to hold hands and say "I love you." Later they have to bear together the burdens of a household, children, and daily life. Their hardships bring them together, without their realizing it. The sorrows of one are those of the other.

"What I wish for is that a Friend be waiting for me on the threshold of the new life to introduce me to the Father. 'See, I haven't lost one of those you entrusted to me, not even this one. I know him, because we've been through various ordeals together.'

"On some occasions I've noticed that the friendship of the One who has wanted to accompany me on the road of life and suffering is a reality. I have only accepted divine love because God has taken the initiative with me. Death itself seems to me a trial in which I shall not be alone.

"I know that it's He who is coming, that I don't have to run, but simply to make room to welcome Him.

"I wanted to give this witness, because God has never disappointed me."

Simon

46

What's the Point of Waiting in these Corridors?

Latin America

There we were, some fifteen of us, straight from our slum. A few grey-haired dads, with their clodhopper gait, turning their felt hats in their hands. Some mothers, weighed down with age before their time, in their best dresses — which are always the same. And of course the urchins, in mama's arms, led by the hand, or clinging to our legs.

But mostly there were young people, girls, very neatly groomed, mostly in trousers, and guys in blue jeans.

One of the boys was carrying our petition in his hand. We had to have water! We had a reservoir in our slum, but the municipality opened the sluices only every week or two, and without notice.

It was a pathetic little petition, lacking the right style, clumsily typed by a typing student on a rented machine. Under the text were dozens of signatures.

The young people were bursting with enthusiasm — and illusions. They knew we were behind them, because we'd discussed the whole thing with our young leader.

I won't soon forget the luxurious corridors of the town hall. We were kicked from office to office like soccer balls.

When a door opened, they would look us up and down, and say: "Wait, the director will be along right away." And we would wait. And wait and wait. Once more. Without any place to sit.

Was I doing the right thing, wasting my time at all these closed doors? I'm a convert. I've met the living Jesus, and I was burning to proclaim Him to my brothers and sisters in the slum. But did that mean waiting in these corridors?

I kept reminding myself that Jesus put himself on a level with ordinary people. His parables were based on their own lives.

What I had to do was clear. I was to try to "read," in our slum, the events of every day with Jesus' eyes. And the every day events today were our lack of water, our helplessness in the face of oppression, and our attitude of "everyone for himself."

Jesus had told me again and again that my suffering neighbor is my sister or brother, and that this sister or brother, in turn, is Himself (Matt 25:40).

My place was right here, then, in the corridors of the town hall. Faith and life intertwine.

Gentlemen in suits and ties passed before our noses, were kow-towed to as "Dr. So-and-So," and never made to wait, whereas we would be losing still another day's pay waiting in these halls.

I can still hear the young mother who encouraged us with, "Jesus was sent from Herod to Pilate, too!" How right she was! Jesus was in last place in life from start to finish. He submitted to the power of the strongest. How could I dare try to make Him known if I refused the last place, side by side with the poor?

Typists in their fashionable outfits would pass by us with little demi-tasses of coffee.

Those coffees... And I thought of the slum, where a mother gets up at five a.m. to feed her children, then stands in line for a bus, in the sun or the rain, and then, if the bus happens to come, spends an hour and a half riding to the factory. When she comes home, simply exhausted, it's eight or nine at night. Sundays she has to do the laundry.

No wonder, then, that so many give up, no longer able to think of anything but sheer survival.

I can't abandon those companions from my slum on the pretext that they're ineffective in the struggle. Human liberation starts at this level — a tender glance or a little service that lightens life's burden. I shall never forget the women who were moved to tears just because I went up to greet them personally.

Finally a Dr. So-and-So was willing to see us. Our young leader read him the petition.

"Water? Once a week? There wouldn't be enough for everyone at once! Impossible! Meanwhile, we'll find some solution or other. In two weeks the problem will be solved." It was said with such conviction that we decided to believe it, once again.

We had already succeeded in some joint actions. But to achieve this isn't everything. The most important thing is to have the experience that we, poor and without rights, can unite. It's to feel that this unity makes us stronger than money and power. We rediscover our dignity.

If we've been cheated today, we'll be back again. There have been occasions when we have come back ten times for the same reason. We'll just do as the widow in the parable did, when she wore down the heartless judge.

But I know I have to be careful. In the parable of the widow, Jesus is not teaching political tactics. He is starting with the widow's situation — which is ours as well. But the purpose was to tell us that's how we should pray without giving up.

It's true, the Gospel is integrated with social and political activity, but it plants a new seed there, the seed of the kingdom of the children of God.

I'm searching for a church with the face of a slum mother I know. While coping with an alcoholic husband, caring for a relative who was very seriously ill, and raising nine children, she adopted an abandoned child, and didn't think twice about it.

In a church like that, Jesus would feel understood.

Anita

47

"We'll miss you"

North America

He's not there! That stood out a mile.

The light of day worked its way into the dismal street of this gigantic city as best it could. The tropical heat, breathless and smoky, stuck to your skin. The iron fire escapes zigzagged uniformly up and down the dirty red walls of the faceless buildings. Police, fire, and ambulance sirens continued to grate on our ears, as they always did, day and night.

He wasn't there.

His old chair was unoccupied. His square yard of sidewalk was empty. He had never left it. The scrawny, dying little tree with the little fence around it seemed so alone, there next to the chair. And the dozen or more garbage cans looked as if they were waiting for someone.

Joe wasn't there.

He had always been there, sitting in his same old brown jacket summer and winter. The jacket had become part of him, just like the old chair. Worn, small and thin, he had a rather round face, always fairly well shaved, and a crown of white hair around his bald pate. He looked sad and lonely, and often seemed to be off in a world of his own. His look was slightly lowered and obscured by thick glasses. He was imperturbable and sparing with words. Faithful to his territory, he never missed a thing, and knew everyone.

I never knew where he slept at night. And where did he get the money for his liquor? Practically everything about him was unknown, including his last name. All you saw was that he was there, all day long, like a sentinel, at the entrance of our block.

"He doesn't bother anybody," you would hear of him. In our neighborhood that's the greatest compliment. We have more than enough fighting and intrigues.

Joe was dead.

Cirrhosis of the liver. Alcoholism. In our neighborhood, all the old men who lived on the sidewalk die of cirrhosis of the liver, if they're not murdered.

Joe's funeral would be on Wednesday at one o'clock. "I'm going," I said to myself. "There probably won't be anybody there but his wife." Joe used to phone her once in a while.

When I got to the funeral home she was indeed there.

But imagine my surprise when I found thirty or so other neighbors from our street! Not one of them that hadn't trouble with another, over skin color, or a woman, or money, or what have you. When you live on top of one another, sparks fly. But today, here were thirty of them all together. I couldn't get over it.

Joe was resting in the middle of the room in an open casket. He wore make-up to make him look as if he were still alive. This is the custom here. He wore an immaculate white shirt, with an impeccable black tie and blue jacket.

Our Joe was not to be recognized! Daniel — five or six years old — cried out, "Joe looks nice today!" "He's in heaven now," a mother explained to her little girl, "where nobody can go. That's why he's dressed up."

After the ceremony we all got on the subway train together for the ride back to our street, laughing and joking.

But why did we all have this feeling that we'd miss Joe? He hadn't seemed to mean anything to anybody, there on his chair. Tomorrow there would be fighting again, and broken bottles would once more litter the streets.

But Joe's death had conjured up the unhoped-for. For *one* afternoon, at least, thirty divided neighbors were reunited. Everybody had said how nice Joe looked and how we'd miss him.

It had taken him quite a while, but he'd worked his little miracle. I still wonder what his secret was.

Was it simply having been there, every day, just there, to watch us?

I walked by his square yard on the sidewalk. A piece of cardboard had been put on the wall of the building, right over the old chair. Someone had written, in ink, "We'll miss you, Joe. Your friends in the neighborhood."

Harry

48

Seduced by a Face

My dear Annette,

You took me by surprise yesterday. In the noise and bustle of the factory it's hard to free your mind up for such serious conversations.

You were trying to grasp the real reasons for my celibacy. They escape you. I seem to you to be a normal man, obliging and sensitive towards women, and not necessarily oblivious to their charms. So, why celibacy?

I'm going to try to explain, but I may not succeed. To understand me you'd have to share my Christian faith.

No, for me celibacy isn't castration, nor is it a selfish turning inward on myself. Actually it's just the opposite.

I've been seduced by a face. More than I could have been by any girl's face in the years of first love. It's the face of Jesus. For me he is the face of God on earth. I have been in love with him, and I still am. For my beloved, I've given up everything. Don't laugh! It's the truth. Take my word for it!

Of course, I've never seen or heard him. He shows his tenderness rather rarely. He's usually a quiet and reserved partner.

But I'm sure he loves me as if I were the only person in the world. At times I've had, as it were, a direct experience of him. And then it's a little like a honeymoon. Everything becomes rosy and easy.

You asked me precise, very personal, almost indiscreet questions and I won't try to sidestep them.

As I told you yesterday, I've known what it is to love a woman. I will go so far as to say that if I hadn't, I wouldn't feel completely normal.

It's daily life which has brought me most often into close contact with certain women, at work and elsewhere. I've spent years in a team with a few young women in the service of the Third World. Like me, they'd chosen celibacy for Jesus' sake.

With one, I had a beautiful friendship, like yours and mine, you might say. For years, there were no problems.

As the days went by, underneath our deep friendship, another, more tender feeling, took root. It was mutual. We weren't naive. If we hadn't consecrated our lives to God, we could have been joined to one another forever.

But we resolved to stay faithful to the God who wanted us for himself alone. The Bible talks about a God who is in his own way jealous and demanding.

It cost us many a battle and many a tear. Believe me, I know what it's like to have a heart that's bleeding.

I won't pretend that we didn't have our weakness. I've nothing of an angel or hero in me, and my heart is made of the same flesh as yours. Surely God, who himself fashioned it for love, understood these weaknesses better than anyone else. But basically we remained faithful, for years.

Then our ways parted. Today, after more than twenty years of separation, we still write to each other.

This beautiful love story was not the only one in my life. There may be people whose hearts are encased in armor, but mine isn't. I've loved other women, too, sometimes secretly, without letting it show, but not without struggles and heartbreak.

I'd like to be able to tell you that I've always been faithful to my vow of celibacy which I made at the age of twenty-five. That would be too beautiful. On such slippery ground as this, I've sometimes fallen and hurt myself.

Yes, Christian voluntary celibacy can be hard. Very hard, sometimes. Especially when God seems far away and unreal. More than once, I've seriously questioned my celibacy.

And yet, as you can see yourself, I'm a happy man. I don't feel frustrated or diminished. My heart, despite the passage of time and several adventures, has remained full of my first love, that of Jesus Christ.

The way I see it, without a great love a man's life is a sad "old maids" life. Without such a love, my option for celibacy wouldn't be worth the trouble.

Take yourself. You've pledged yourself to one man for life. You're supposed to be faithful to him even if he were far away, and rarely gave any signs of life. This too can be terribly demanding at times.

You know I wouldn't want our friendship to encroach the least bit on the love you have for your husband. Not for all the world!

Our friendship must be — and it is — like that of a sister and brother.

This is the only way my heart, a brother's heart, God's property, can stay free.

I want to confide to you too that, every day, I spend long moments in silent prayer before this God. Without this heart-to-heart, I think — in fact I'm sure — I'd never have been able to hold out.

There! Now I've passed my secret on to you.

Peter

49
Christmas in Boston?

At sea

December 22

12 noon.   We're only twenty-four hours from Boston. Our freighter is near the end of this Atlantic crossing loaded with European cars.

Where will we celebrate Christmas? At sea? Ashore? German, Austrian, or Spaniard, each of us wonders. For all of us, Christmas has stayed sacred somehow. You miss your family more than ever. Christmas should never be celebrated on a ship.

If all goes well, we should leave Boston in time to spend Christmas in the next port.

8 p.m.   A sudden storm. We've slowed down. The wind from Labrador is icy cold.

Midnight.   I'm going on watch. Four hours. The night's a black one. The ship's dancing like a cork.

December 23

4 a.m.   Back down to my cabin. I'll try to get some kind of rest. The ship is creaking all over. Where will we celebrate Christmas?

7 a.m.   Daybreak. The storm is over, as suddenly as it began. A beam of sunshine has even dropped in to say hello.

The vessel's turned into a ghost ship. Spray has frozen everywhere: warps, capstan, derricks, winches and lifting gear. The bridge is gleaming like a mirror.

Captain shouting, "All hands on deck!" With big, heavy gloves on, we struggle to melt everything off with hot water and steam jets.

Would we celebrate Christmas in Boston?

1 p.m.   Here we are, steaming slowly into the port. The city is all white, under a blue sky. There's mail for us. We start unloading the cars.

6 p.m.   The stevedores don't work overtime at night. The sky is threatening, and work has stopped. Looks like Christmas in Boston.

Little groups of us make a tour of the snow-covered town. As is the custom here, candles are burning in practically every window. Everywhere there are Christmas trees with brightly colored lights on them. Bostonians are busy with their last-minute shopping. You feel a little twinge in your heart.

We buy a few souvenirs for our families, down a beer, then back on board.

December 24

7 a.m.   A foot and a half of powdery snow covers everything. And it's still coming down. The weather is milder. Now it's almost sure: we'll be celebrating Christmas in Boston.

Noon. The snow has stopped. The captain and the dock foremen are having a meeting.

"All hands on deck!" Again! This time it's to sweep the snow off to open the holds. Snowplows will do the same on the quay. So long, Christmas in Boston! We're all grumbling. On the pier they're working like crazy. They've got a bonus, and they're trying to finish in time to be home for Christmas Eve.

8 p.m. The last car has been unloaded. The dock workers are jumping into their cars. In a few minutes the quay is deserted. Two tugboats are already here to take us out to sea. Nobody here cares about us, that's for sure. We don't have the courage to grumble.

Twelve hours to the next port. Will it be the traditional Christmas at sea? A beautifully prepared meal, the Christmas Gospel read by a volunteer, and presents from evangelical missions and the ship's owner? Right now, ashore, everyone is starting Christmas Eve.

"All hands in the hold!" At the next port we'll be taking on coal, so all the ramps where the cars were stacked have to be pulled down. It's dangerous and very tiring. I'm not assigned to this work because I have the midnight watch.

It's almost midnight. The sea's getting very rough. The work in the hold has to stop. Some of the men are saying, "It's Christmas!"

December 25

Midnight. Time to go on watch. A real storm. In the empty ship everything seems about to break. They'll be hanging on to their bunks down there. We were all hoping to celebrate Christmas eating and drinking. Deep down, it's something else we wish for, but we don't mention that.

I'm thinking of the shepherds of Bethlehem. I think about them everytime I spend Christmas at sea. I remind myself that the Happening was announced to very simple people right where they were, right on the job. And they rose up with joyful hearts.

For us, the Happening came when we were in the hold. The inexpressible longing for a little real joy won't go away.

This night watch did me good.

9 a.m.   There's the port. We stay moored. Rain and melting snow. The captain sends us down to finish the dismantling in the hold. We'll be paid double time, he says. To hell with double time! It will never replace Christmas.

Here we are down here, sad and bitter. Icy rain comes down on us through the open hatches.

I bring down a box of chocolates. You have to do something for Christmas. We pass it around, standing up, soaked through, with our faces as dark as the chocolate.

Roger

50

Evening Prayer

South of the Sahara

Evening is a marvelous time.

I'd just sat down, with my back against the wall of the hut. On this mound I was waiting for nightfall, facing the sun which was setting behind the hills.

The landscape was scorched, desperate-looking. It was summer. Thin, bluish smoke hung over a nearby hamlet. In a little valley, a small stream sprang singing from rock to rock. Just listening to it was refreshing.

Along the paths, men were returning from the fields, their hoes on their shoulders. A young man was coming back from town on his motorbike, disturbing the silence. A group of women passed by, single file, each with an enormous load of wood on her head. You felt they were too tired to talk.

The sun slid rapidly out of sight. In the space of a few moments a great calm settled over everything. All fell silent, the birds in the trees, the animals moving unseen in the brush. Nature was at prayer.

I felt silence within myself.

Suddenly, the Muslim call to prayer rose in the distance. I get the same feeling every time I hear it. In this setting, surrounded by nature and stillness, this moment had something unique about it.

> God is great!
> There is no God but God!

Night had fallen. Back in the hut, I lit the kerosene lamp and began my evening vigil before the face of my God.

> And the Word was made flesh,
> and dwelt among us.

I offered God all those bent backs, all those arms weary of swinging their picks. I remembered all the smiles, glances and greetings which had been exchanged.

> "May your day pass in peace!"
> "Peace before you!"
> "Peace behind you!"

They were all there with me, this evening, those who were thirsting for peace. Thirsting to know the Utterly Other and the Utterly Near!

Surely God must start when the hearts of his children all turn toward Him together!

Olive